RISJ *CHALLENGES*

Between Commodification and Lifestyle Politics

Does Silvio Berlusconi provide a New Model of Politics for the Twenty-First Century?

Paolo Mancini

REUTERS INSTITUTE for the STUDY of JOURNALISM

UNIVERSITY OF OXFORD

Contents

Executive Summary

A new style of politics emerged at the end of the twentieth century which fundamentally changes both the assumptions and the practices of political contestation as experienced in the Western democracies in the nineteenth and twentieth centuries.

The shift to the new politics has been deeply influenced by the media, and by the politicians' need to master the media and public relations techniques which the new style of mass politics presses upon them. One of the most extreme versions of this mastery of the media as a political tool is to be found in the figure and in the governing style of Silvio Berlusconi, three times Prime Minister of Italy and the billionaire owner of most of the country's commercial TV channels, the largest publishing house, largest advertising agency and several important newspapers.

Berlusconi came into politics in 1993/4, creating a new party – Forza Italia, now Popolo della Liberta – financed by him and staffed by executives of his advertising agency, Pubblitalia. His media companies, which had been relatively independent, were then instructed to support his political ventures – developing a 'presidentialist' style of government.

This new style of politics came into being in part because political parties everywhere in the democratic world were losing members and power, and politicians were turning more and more to the mass media to get their messages across. Citizens are now treated increasingly as an audience as much as an electorate – an approach which the Berlusconi governments have greatly furthered.

Berlusconi's power lies not just in his wealth and the influence of his media, but in the values he promotes. Television remains the most powerful medium for the population, and is experienced as part of everyday life. The link with the everyday media experiences of the population, and the promotion of the values of entertainment and consumption, has given the Italian Prime Minister powerful support.

Berlusconi's political power is further bolstered by his character and actions – he has enjoyed playing the parts both of a showman and of someone who is 'ordinary' and who has the same reactions, desires and even prejudices of the man in the street. Until recently, his sexual escapades have been seen as enviable rather than culpable.

Although the Italian Prime Minister is the outstanding example of the politician as media manipulator, he should not be seen as a lone exception. The structural constraints on contemporary politicians and the desires of other leading political figures to play something of the same role as Berlusconi mean that he has imitators – chief among whom is the French President, Nicolas Sarkozy. The collapse of the grand narratives promulgated by political parties in the nineteenth and twentieth centuries point the political class ineluctably along the path mapped out by the Prime Minister of Italy.

Introduction: Conventional Wisdom

The society that has been created by television is naturally a society of the right. It is the society of Sanremo Music Festival, sport, TV commercials, Pippo Baudo, Mike Buongiorno, Beautiful and so on. It is not Berlusconi who won, it is the society that his mass media organizations have created that won. This is the society that enjoys looking at stupid families sitting around a table celebrating this or that product.[1] (N. Bobbio, 1994)

This essay argues against what I like to define as the conventional wisdom on Silvio Berlusconi. Mainly among foreign journalists, commentators and scholars who observe the Italian political scene from outside, there is a widely shared opinion that Berlusconi won the elections in 1994, and (until recently) continued to win elections, because he owns the major commercial television corporation, together with important dailies and weeklies. This conventional wisdom goes on to point out that Berlusconi is involved in a dramatic conflict of interests – being at the same time Prime Minister and an entrepreneur with business interests in different areas in which the government has to make crucial decisions. And again: much of the power (and much of the wealth) Berlusconi holds comes from a close relationship with mafia and other criminal groups. Finally on conventional wisdom: it holds that Berlusconi has identified, and identified with, the stereotype of the Italian man: a womaniser, brilliant, amiable and jokey. This is what I see as the conventional wisdom about the Italian Prime Minister. A large literature exists both in Italian and in English that reinforces this (Veltri and Travaglio, 2001; Bocca, 2002; Sylos Labini, 2003; Ginsborg, 2004; Stille, 2006; Miller-Jones, 2011).

---

[1] Sanremo festival is a very well-known music festival, broadcast live for the past fifty years; Pippo Baudo and Mike Bongiorno are famous TV personalities and *Beautiful* a very successful soap opera.

I believe that what this conventional wisdom suggests is substantially correct. I believe it gives a true picture of the past two decades. Nevertheless, it also seems to me that it represents a restrictive and partial reading of the political figure of Berlusconi; I would argue that he represents an instance of the massive changes in the relationship of politics to the media in many countries, including but not limited to it. Beyond the exoticism and the eccentricity that the figure of Berlusconi may embody, together with all the conflicts that he may provoke, he represents the prototype of a new structure of politics and a new form of the involvement of people with the problems and the ruling of the community. In short, the thesis I want to suggest here is the following: Berlusconi represents 'the end of old politics'. The new politics (already in place in Italy, less so in other countries for reasons I shall discuss later on) is determined and framed by television. Television with its messages, values and view of the world, interferes continuously with politics and determines and shapes its values. A political universe abstracted and separated from television seems to be no longer possible. I have to stress also that what I am describing here can take place in different ways and levels depending on contextual, national factors, some of which I shall try to outline in the Italian case.

Many in Italy talk about 'the exceptionalism' and the 'anomaly' of Berlusconi, stressing how he represents a degeneration of contemporary politics as, among other negative features, he represents an exaggerated version of modern populism. In this case too, these observations well describe aspects of his political style; yet they, too, underestimate the dramatic changes that he represents.

I want to demonstrate that Berlusconi is not a transitory phenomenon: that he represents and identifies an important change in the forms of politics and of political involvement that go beyond the contingencies of his personal history, with all the contradictions and problems that this personal history may involve.

1. Which Theoretical Tool Frames the Berlusconi Experience?

A new form of politics?

Berlusconi embodies the end of politics as it has been experienced in the nineteenth and twentieth centuries – what one might call 'old' politics. He is a vivid example of how we are entering an era of 'new' politics that I shall try to describe, using him and the Italian case as my examples.

Those who underline the 'anomaly' of Berlusconi's populism believe that democracy could be exempt from the phenomena which authors such as Daniel Bell (1960), Jean-Francois Lyotard (1979) Francis Fukuyama (1992) and many other have described. These are very different authors with different theoretical approaches who have a similar thesis: all of them stress the end (it is not by chance that the word 'end' is used in the titles of the books of two of these authors), or at least the dramatic weakening, of those frameworks that, during the last two centuries, have represented the symbolic 'cement' of the mass parties that have been an important feature of modern European history.

The political systems of Western democracies in the last two centuries – communism, socialism, Catholicism, liberalism – have been rooted in these general symbolic frameworks. Today these frameworks, where they still exist, are much weaker, and are much less able to motivate citizens and to offer them good and convincing motives to get together and to take an active part in the life of the community (this is not, of course, just an Italian problem: it concerns all Western democracies). The mass parties which embody these symbolic constructions are undergoing a dramatic change – together with all the different forms of political participation that up to now were organised essentially around similar collective organisations of a very stable nature. Obvious examples of this tendency can be found in the experience of most of the Socialist and Catholic parties in the Western world, in the experience of most of the unions, etc. Recent episodes in the Mediterranean area also demonstrate that today political action is in hands of movements - groups, more or less spontaneous and essentially depending on the use of the internet, that have very little in common with the traditions, the values, the imagery of the mass parties that shaped Western history over the past two centuries.

The hypotheses which stress Berlusconian exceptionalism underestimate the fact that an historical period has ended: the period during which a specific version of politics was dominant, built around the deeply rooted symbolic constructions of mass parties born in the nineteenth century and developed through the twentieth century in Western democracies.

Berlusconi, I believe, is an example – in dramatic and exotic terms, and in a specific relationship to the Italian national context – of this shift from 'old' to 'new politics'. I believe this shift cannot be hidden behind the conventional wisdom which stresses only the most obvious, 'Italian' nature of the visible changes taking place.

To show this, I want to suggest that 'Berlusconi may not be alone': all around the world, with different features, there are many other cases and examples that point up very similar sets of changes. The ideas that I will try to outline here derive from my reading of studies of the brief political experience of Pym Fortuyn in the Netherlands – 'a Dandy in politics' as Pels defines him (2003); research on the success and then the fall and imprisonment of Lord Archer in Great Britain (Corner, 2003); the existing similarities between Sarkozy and Berlusconi (Musso, 2008; Campus, 2010); investigations into the increasing personalisation of politics, particularly evident in the case of Tony Blair (Langer, 2007). The description that Dick Pels gives of the brief political adventure of Pym Fortuyn works perfectly for Berlusconi. Just change the name of the country and you have the perfect image of the first years of 'Il Cavaliere' as political actor:

> *Suddenly politics in the Netherlands had turned into an exciting 'fun' thing, whipping up unheard-of popular passions; everyone was talking politics and everywhere Fortuyn occupied the center of attention. A series of televised campaign debates between the major political leaders turned into a regular soap opera in which the cheeky superstar repeatedly exposed the reigning LabLib elite*

as a bunch of old men by his charming but often ad hominem provocations – while conspicuously failing to answer any of the disturbing questions. (Pels, 2003: 42)

These studies, most of which come under the label of either popularisation of politics (van Zoonen, 2005; Riegert, 2007; Mazzoleni and Sfardini, 2009) or celebrity politics (Marshall, 1997) confirm that the change I am talking about here is more widespread and general. As they show, there is an increasing interchange between popular culture and politics, mostly determined by the increasing role of the mass media, and television in particular, as agents of political socialisation.

The idea of a 'popularisation of politics' is found in the previous works of several pioneers, who had already noticed how *politics* and *spectacle* were progressively overlapping. Indeed, the works on 'political spectacle' by scholars such as Debord (1967) and Schwartzenberg (1977) and their followers had already pointed out that the way in which political actors try to involve citizens in political action has changed over the years, giving rise to a wide spectrum of different forms of political dramatisation. The seminal works by Murray Edelman (1971, 1976, 1977) stressed the importance of the symbolic dimension in politics, underestimated in most of the previous analysis of politics and political communication. Recently much attention has been devoted to populism by both political scientists and media scholars (Meny and Surel, 2002); to neo-populism (Mazzoleni *et al.*, 2003) and to telepopulism (Peri, 2004); according to these authors, many political leaders in different parts of the world have clearly demonstrated this populist dimension. More recently, several analyses have been devoted to the so-called mediatisation of politics (Mazzoleni and Schulz, 1999), stressing the changes that are taking place because of the increasing role of the mass media in the relationship between politics, political actors and citizens.

All these studies, mainly by media scholars, underline important and dramatic changes. Yet their defect is that they envisage these shifts as acting at either a specific, or generally superficial, level leaving the conception of politics and democracy unchanged either because what these studies underline relates to the way in which politics is represented and communicated (this is the case of the works on spectacularisation of politics and its mediatisation) or they assume that there exists some sort of 'good' politics which today may easily degenerate into populism (Campus, 2006).

These studies miss the central point: that is, the ending of nineteenth- and twentieth-century politics based on the essential role of organised political parties, with their values, dreams, aspirations, images of adversaries. They do not see that politics is changing because the context of citizens' everyday lives is changing, as are their cultural consumption and their habits of socialisation. New forms of politics need to be linked to the disappearance of those cleavages around which the political struggles of the two previous centuries took place, and which gave birth to mass parties. Today there are new forms of involvement, as Peter Dahlgren wrote: 'Postmodern politics is increasingly marked by a lack of commitment to traditional institutions such as political parties, labour unions and civic associations, yet composed of temporary alliance around issues and values linked to everyday life (such as morality, identity and worldview)' (Dahlgren, 2000: 318). Berlusconi represents a specific case of a temporary alliance built around a specific set of values, images and dreams that connect everyday life to politics, and have little to do with the set of motives that used to determine political participation.

Political scientists have long studied the modifications in the forms of democracy and politics. Most of them have underlined the progressive weakening of political parties and their shift towards different functions – in large part seen as happening in response to the increasing importance of the mass media as agents of political socialisation (Mair, 1990; Katz and Mair, 1994). They have stressed how the structures of the mass parties are changing, as well as their relationship with government on one side and with citizens on the other, and their tendency to become 'cartel parties', that is, decreasing the level of competition with other parties with which they construct more or less stable alliances, increasing in this way the self-referentiality of politics. As already noted, other scholars have pointed out how, in face of the progressive disappearance of stable connections both of a symbolic and structural nature between mass parties and citizens, neo-populism has increased (Meny and Surel, 2002), leaving room for the birth of new forms of 'personal parties' established around the figure of single politicians. In particular this has been studied in connection with the Italian and Berlusconi experience (Fabbrini, 1999; Calise, 2000).

The seminal work of Otto Kirkheimer (1966) on the 'catch-all party' has already pointed out the lack of ideology that characterises the evolution of West European political parties which abandon their traditional constituencies. This is clearly manifest in Berlusconi's 'Forza Italia' party, with its close involvement with media and advertising professionals, that was foreshadowed in the concept of the 'electoral-professional party' that

Angelo Panebianco saw as a new frontier in the evolution of modern mass parties (Panebianco, 1988).

The experience of Berlusconi in government clearly confirms the tendency towards presidentialisation that many authors have noted in different parts of the world (Mugham, 2000; Poguntke and Webb, 2005). Both personalisation and presidentialisation confirm Manin's thesis on audience democracy – to be discussed later – where he places a strong emphasis on the increasing importance of single politicians dominating all political initiatives.

In the political experience of the present Italian Prime Minister, national features mix with the kind of social and political shifts which a large literature, both in the field of media studies and political science, has highlighted. As Paul Ginsborg, a well-known British scholar of Italian history, suggests, we may regard Berlusconi as an exception but also as a 'prototype' (Ginsborg, 2004): after describing a large number of problems emerging in democracy worldwide (personalisation of power, the diffusion of the figure of media mogul, the overlapping between politics and entertainment, the many billionaires entering the field of politics), Ginsborg concludes:

> *Silvio Berlusconi represents the Italian declination of these trends. His is the most ambitious attempt to date to combine media control and political power. He is the first of these figures to lead a major nation state, ranked seventh in the world in economic terms. We may choose to regard him as a prototype or as an exception, and time will tell which of these views is closer to the truth. In either case, his trajectory is significant and worthy of being studied in depth.* (Ginsborg, 2004: 10)

In this book I am choosing to look at Berlusconi as 'a prototype' – as a new possible model of politics that is already visible in Italy, and that may become more important in other countries as well.

In a recent article in the Italian journal *Internazionale*, the deputy editor of *El Pais*, Lluis Bassets, puts forward, in strong language, the thesis that clearly confirms the sort of 'universalistic' character I want to emphasise:

> *The malign figure of Berlusconi has been for the Italian and European politics what Attila has been with his Huns: he has modified the landscape of politics and mass media. As the Catalan*

*writer and journalist Antoni Puigverd has written, 'The imago
mundi of popular classes is now that of Telecinco (the Spanish TV
channel owned by Berlusconi's Mediaset corporation)[2]*

This brings us back to Bobbio's epigraph that opens this volume: it
highlights a process of change that has a very general character, involving
different aspects of social life. It concerns the nature of cultural
consumption, the structures of political participation, the forms of political
communication and the attitudes and behaviour of citizens towards
problems of general interest, together with the disappearing boundaries
between private and public life. Much of this has to do with the role of the
mass media and television in particular.

Bernard Manin's 'audience democracy'

Ilvo Diamanti, a leading Italian political scientist, has pointed out
(Diamanti, 2010) that Bernard Manin's theory of 'audience democracy'
seems an appropriate theoretical box within which to insert Berlusconi's
political experience. As we shall see later, there are other possible
theoretical frameworks that could be used: but Manin's hypothesis seems
very adequate in this regard (Manin, 1997). First, his idea of audience
democracy explains the present forms of politics in an historical
perspective and is thus particularly useful for understanding the changes
that have taken place (de Beus, 2011). Second, Manin offers a more
comprehensive view than other existing theoretical interpretations. Indeed
his view is not limited to one part of the political process; he surveys the
overall framework of politics – including politicians, citizens and mass
media – allowing his interpretation to offer the possibility of observing the
changes from both an institutional and from a 'process' point of view.

Jos de Beus, in his discussion of Manin's thesis, observes:

*pioneers of audience democracy include the German chancellor
Gerhard Schroder, the Italian prime minister Silvio Berlusconi
and the Dutch parliamentary candidate Pim Fortuyn (all of
whom were active in multi-party settings) and, in the two-party
settings of the UK and US, Prime Minister Tony Blair, President
Bill Clinton, presidential candidate Ross Perot and Arnold
Schwarzenegger, Governor of California. (de Beus, 2011: 31)*

---

[2] L. Bassets, 'Il berlusconismo ha già vinto', *Internazionale*, 901 (10–16 June 2011).

Several of these names have already been quoted in the previous pages in relationship to the dramatisation and mediatisation of politics. Further cases may also be understood in the light of Manin's thesis.

Manin proposes three types of government in a representative democracy: parliamentarianism, party democracy and audience democracy. Contemporary democracies, he says, are characterised by a shift from parliamentarism, which was then replaced by party democracy in the last century, to audience democracy today. Three main features of his hypothesis seem to be a particularly useful prism through which to view the Berlusconi phenomenon.

First, Manin emphasises how, in audience democracy, the mass media substitute themselves for the political parties as the main agents of political socialisation: in his view, mass media are not just the main providers of information towards citizens – that is, they are not just news media – they also represent the principal forum for political discussion and deliberation. Berlusconi is the most evident instance of this tendency. He established the new party 'Forza Italia' in January 1994 and won his first election in April of the same year without an organisational structure of the traditional type, and without any important support by followers and party members. His success was due to the mass media, and television in particular; Berlusconi used, massively, his own television channels, but relied also on the wide attention he was able to command within the entire mass media system, because of the novelty he represented. This, too, is a departure from the conventional wisdom, which limits its attribution of his success to the use he made of his Mediaset conglomerate. Being the owner of the main commercial television conglomerate has been and remains an important element of his success, and there is no doubt that, especially in the 1994 campaign, a very large number of political commercials were aired on Mediaset channels to promote his new party and his personality. But this is just one part of the story: in 1994 Berlusconi was able to capture, daily, the attention of the news media, including of those media opposed to him, by offering appealing news stories, and thus was able to occupy the centre of the political scene. He was the main news story every night – an ability which he retains, for good and ill, to this day. He appears before the electorate as the first choice; whether that choice is taken or rejected, all the competitors appear as secondary figures.

Many studies have, at different times and occasions, demonstrated this. For much of the 2006 political election campaign he was well behind his opponent, Prodi, in all the existing opinion polls; in the last fifteen days of the campaign, however, he was able to keep himself, uninterruptedly, at the centre of the mass media stage – launching a number of different initiatives, making provocative and unexpected statements. For fifteen days he was *the* news story in each newscast. In this way he was able to dramatically diminish the gap between him and Prodi: he lost, but by only 25,000 votes (Mancini, 2007). It is worth remembering that on that occasion (as in all election campaigns after 1994) the use of political ads was not permitted, and a strict law controlled the distribution of airtime. His success in closing the gap between himself and his opponent was essentially a matter of successful news making, which drew attention away from Prodi, the front-runner, towards himself and his own proposals.

Even today, Il Popolo della Libertà (PdL) – Berlusconi's new party, which replaced Forza Italia at the end of 2007 – doesn't have any real, decentralised diffused organisation, nor any important decision-making structure. The elements that featured strongly in the traditional mass parties have no place in Forza Italia or the PdL – both characterised by weak organisation, few members, few branches, no fixed procedures for the decision-making process and very weak intermediary bodies between the leader and party members and voters. The change of the name of the party is itself a clear indicator of the very weak symbolic identity of the party Berlusconi established. This change was made without debate within the party organisation: the decision was taken by the leader without any consultation with the members and the affiliated. This demonstrates how the PdL is rooted in the figure of Berlusconi himself, and in the values and dreams he embodies. The party relies almost entirely on the mass media, and television in particular, as the means to reach the citizens: journalists refer to it as a 'plastic party'. Absent the mass membership and organising ability of a conventional party, the mass media represent the only possible way to spread information, to establish a symbolic identity rooted in a system of values embodied by the leader himself.

The importance Manin gives to 'personalities at the expense of platforms' (Manin, 1997: 220) is the second main feature in his audience democracy theory. Representative government in such a system relies on a single political figure much more than in previous forms of democracy. The personalisation of political communication, and of political power in general, that today represents a common feature of many Western democracies, is extreme in the case of Berlusconi: the very weak structure of his party forces a focus on his personality, while the decision-making processes of both the party and the government, together with most of the symbolic values with which the party identifies, are also centred on him.

The idea of the 'personal party', discussed at length by Mauro Calise (2000) and others in Italy (e.g. Fabbrini, 1999) and elsewhere, features audience democracy in an important way. Berlusconi is not just the television figure before everyone's eyes every night – Manin calls this '*the media figure*' (1997: 220) – he is also the one who established a party around his own figure and role. The party relies almost exclusively on his personal resources, both economic and symbolic. There is no other individual within the party organisation who, now or in the foreseeable future, could replace him. There is no important, decisive debate: the party leader does not face any internal opposition. 'The personal party' has a more or less complete absence of important and stable platforms and strong policy issues.

In Manin's thesis, trust is an indispensable dimension of the personalisation of political power: 'the personal trust that the candidate inspires is a more adequate basis of selection than the evaluation of plans for future actions' (1997: 221). The figure of the single politician and the trust he is able to gain are indispensable resources of audience democracy and, of course, they are linked to the role of the mass media and television in particular in connecting the political leader to citizens. Indeed the previous statement by Manin confirms and reinforces what Kurt and Gladys Lang, with others, had already noticed in 1956, when they wrote that the television personality 'is judged solely in terms of its appropriateness for TV, independently of its political import' (Lang and Lang, 1956: 104).

Manin doesn't specify what he means by 'trust', referring instead to the work of John Dunn on political responsibility. Dunn writes: 'Trust as a human passion may rest on close familiarity or massive social distance. Many have trusted their Queen (or Stalin) as implicitly as ever they have trusted their spouse or favourite sibling' (1990: 27). This is a central point in our examination of Berlusconi: in his case, trust (the confidence he is able to inspire in his followers and voters) is very different from most traditional political faith. Trust in Berlusconi is essentially an 'extra-political' trust: it has little to do with the traditional values, cleavages and issues of political and ideological debate, but is constructed on categories that appear to be taken essentially from everyday life. The trust which people invest in the present Italian Prime Minister has many of the same facets as trust in a spouse or favourite sibling; Berlusconi has been able to embody values and aspirations that are part of everyday life, composed of the feelings, passions and dreams of a large part of Italian population. As we shall see, the level of *traditional* political trust in Berlusconi is generally low (at least compared to that of his competitor, Prodi, in the 2006 elections): this appears to mean that the present Italian Prime Minister is judged and trusted less as a politician of the traditional kind, but that the levels of trust he does inspire in his supporters rely to a great extent on everyday experiences and feelings.

A third element in Manin's view of audience democracy is what he defines as the 'initiative': in his view, this aspect appears to be still more important than those I have highlighted above. Indeed, Manin stresses that, in audience democracy, the 'terms of electoral choice belongs to politicians and not to the electorate' (1997: 223). The single political figure does offer platforms to the electorate, but it is composed of values and images in which the voter is requested to recognise himself. In the previous forms of democracy – parliamentary and party – there were strong contributions by actors other than the single political figure, who assisted and sometimes led in constructing and defining electoral platforms. In audience democracy, voters are mere spectators of that which is put on the stage by those politicians who are the initiators and the central, dominant figures. Audience democracy is made up by a receptive public, a 'reactive public' in Manin's words; in the previous model, the initiative was also in the hands of citizens, party organisations, organised social interests, and there was a pattern, involving different social actors, according to which political platforms were constructed, negotiated, and even changed. Citizens were an active part of the decision-making process.

Manin's 'initiative' thesis is similar to the many studies and interpretations of scholars of the media and symbolism, who have stressed the more and more spectacular character of today's political performances. Indeed, the thesis of *spectacularisation* or *dramatisation* of politics stresses the essentially receptive role of the citizens in front of the 'mise en scene' derived from the initiatives of the political world. The seminal works by Debord (1967), Schwartzenberg (1977) and more recently by Meyer (2002) and others, all point out the transformation from a community of active citizens to a community of passive spectators. Manin recaps these hypotheses, and sets them in a more comprehensive, political science-inspired, framework.

There is no doubt that Berlusconi is an 'initiator': his entire political design is based on the claim that his personal skills make him uniquely competent to run the government. From the electoral campaign of 1994, he put before Italian voters the image of a rich, clever entrepreneur who had created a very profitable and efficient enterprise, who owns one of the most famous and successful football teams, AC Milan, and who can therefore adapt for use in politics the principles of business efficiency and profitability that he applied so successfully to his enterprises. Since 1994 Berlusconi has always kept the political initiative, constantly arguing that 'I have the solution for that problem', not delegating the role of problem-solver to anyone else, except in a secondary role. One prominent example: in the case of the Naples garbage crisis at the beginning of his most recent premiership, he went to the city, ordering the entire government to meet there and personally promising to solve the problem within a month. It seemed, at first, that he had: though the problem soon recurred (and remains unsolved, and larger than ever, to this day).

Another example: after the earthquake in the city of L'Aquila in April 2009, he moved the G8 summit from a remote resort in Sardinia to the very centre of the partially destroyed region of Abruzzi, a decision on which there was neither discussion nor consultation with his G8 partners. Finally: when illegal immigrants began arriving in large numbers in the spring of 2011 on the Sicilian island of Lampedusa, he flew to the island and said that 'I promise, within three days, there will not be any immigrants left on this island', adding 'to show that I'm serious on this, I must tell you that I have just bought a house on your island'. The last claim was false (he bought a house on the island much later): but most of the immigrants were, in fact, moved on.

Berlusconi's political career has been marked by many such episodes, in which *he* assumes personal responsibility: *he* is the person who can solve the problems, *he* the one who has the solution to propose in front of a receptive audience. Indeed one of his flattering nicknames, and the one he most likes, is 'L'uomo della provvidenza' (the man touched by God): such a man must have the solution for all problems.

This role has as perhaps its most important dimension a symbolic power – and the ability to command the media stage. Since 1994 Berlusconi has been the main 'story' for the Italian mass media. He has been able to catch the attention of news organisations not just as the owner of the major private networks – as the conventional wisdom theory states – but as the political figure who offers to news organisations stories tailored to attract the interest of the widest audience. He knows, both intuitively and through his media experience, what symbolic material attracts an audience and wins attention in a competitive, market-driven, mass media system.

Other possible theoretical frameworks

Manin's thesis is supplemented by the work of Edward Green, whose book, *The Eyes of the People*, notes the shift from a democracy based on debate and therefore on 'the voice', to a democracy of the eyes – 'today, citizens are not, most of the time, decision makers, relating to politics with their voice, but spectators who relate to politics with their eyes' (Green, 2010: 4). For Green, political debate is continuously losing ground: citizens take less and less part in discussions about public affairs. Instead they limit themselves to watching what is put on the public stage by political actors. These two authors argue that the mass media have caused a shift, not just in communication strategies, but in the essence of the democratic experience itself; they have identified an essential shift in the process of political socialisation that causes those structures and procedures that previously regulated political life to wither.

F. R. Ankersmit uses the concept of 'aesthetic politics' to argue how, in contemporary democracy, politics is more and more dependent on its representation. Political philosophy, he says, recognises how the real world of political activity exists, for most people, only insofar as it is represented to citizens. Drawing on works as diverse as those of Macchiavelli and Murray Edelman, Ankersmit points out the importance of representation, that which he defines as the 'aesthetic' dimension of politics. Berlusconi has paid a lot of attention to different 'aesthetic' devices: he is always accompanied by his personal beautician, his hair has been transplanted, while the PdL, Partito della Libertà (Freedom Party) textbooks on campaigning stress the importance of the right clothes to wear in different situations. Berlusconi's entire political proposal is deeply affected by 'aestheticism'.

2. The Berlusconi Imagery

From First to Second Republic

Berlusconi, as I have noted, embodies many of the elements described above. To foreign observers, these often appear as a mixture of exoticism and unconventionality, together with frequent dishonesty and political incorrectness. To many Italian observers these appear even more negative – because they contrast them with the previous political culture of Italy.

Audience democracy needs spectators: usually they are citizens unused to taking an active part in political life. These citizens sit, as it were, in a theatre, waiting to watch the 'initiator' on the stage. The spectators essentially want to be entertained (this is usually the reason one buys a theatre ticket) and they expect to be surprised and fascinated by the person acting on the stage. 'Apathy' is the word that Murray Edelman used to define 'most of the world's population, even most of the population of the advanced countries, that has no incentive to define joy, failure or hope in terms of public affairs' (Edelman, 1988: 7). The public of an audience democracy is indifferent – and indifference means that it does not have deeply rooted political opinions.

> *The public is mainly a black hole into which the political efforts of politicians, advocates of causes, the media, and the schools disappear with hardly a trace. Its apathy, indifference, quiescence and resistance to the consciousness industry is especially impressive in an age of widespread literacy and virtually universal access to the media.* (Edelman, 1988: 8)

Edelman wrote these statements in 1988; they have proved applicable to the emergence of an Italian leader some years later. Before 1994, the year

Berlusconi decided to enter the political arena, the apathy level in Italy was not, relatively speaking, high: most citizens had an already well-established opinion about politics. Even if most of them didn't take an active part in political life, still voting levels were among the highest in Europe, and the level of party membership was similarly high.

For almost fifty years there was no important shift in Italian elections. Citizens would generally vote for the same party; after the end of fascism in 1945, the Christian Democratic party was the single largest party and took on the main responsibility for government (together with some allied parties); and the Communist Party became and remained the main opposition party. Shifts in the number of votes each party received did occur, but they were relatively minor.

Political scientists attribute this long stability of the Italian electoral scene to what they define as the 'affiliation vote': citizens were linked (and still are partially linked) to party organisations by firm, well-rooted ideological and cultural ties; very frequently these links were also of a clientelistic nature. They were mostly the product of established habits deriving from individual and family experience, rooted in the specific tradition of the group to which each voter belonged and in the personal interactions taking place within this group (Parisi and Pasquino, 1977). Political attachments and opinions were often seen as existing on the level of a religion: not to be betrayed.

Children from a Catholic family were often sent to a Catholic school, were encouraged to read Catholic newspapers, and the entire environment (friends, relatives, clubs, sport organisations) within which they grew up was close to the Catholic Church – and thus the decision to vote for the Christian Democratic, or Catholic, party was almost a natural one. Choices made outside of that environment were not frequent. The same may largely apply to the environment around the competing Communist Party; indeed, many have observed that, for decades, Italy has been divided into two main subcultures, the so-called red one (socialist and communist) and the white one (Catholic culture) (Trigilia, 1981). The first was strong in the central regions of Italy – Emilia-Romagna, Tuscany, Umbria and the Marche – while the second spread across the eastern and northern regions, as well as in the south. The situation was in some measure analogous to that in the Netherlands; there, the country was divided into three main subcultures: Catholic, Protestant and Liberal-Socialist, which controlled a significant part of the socialisation process, and was able to ensure electoral stability.

In this framework, the party was the main force: *it* was the patron, not any single politician. The main relationship, at least in Central and Northern Italy, was between single members of the subculture and its general cultural and symbolic framework. What counted was the feeling that 'this is my world' and not 'this is my beloved leader' – even if the figure of the leader often carried major importance. Something very close to 'religious faith' brought together the members of each cultural and ideological community: and cutting religious links is not easy. There were deep cultural and ideological fractures, deeply contrasting interests existing among the different parties, among the parties within the same government coalition, and within the parties themselves: yet for a period of almost fifty years of post-fascist history, the same people and the same parties ran the Italian government.

This long-lasting stability was completely overthrown by the events of 1992–3 during which the old political world was destroyed: following the 'Mani pulite' (clean hands) or 'Tangentopoli' (bribery city) processes, many leading political figures were arrested and their political organisations were found to be so immersed in the scandals that, little by little, they were wholly or largely destroyed. The general secretary of the Socialist Party, Benito Craxi, was accused of corruption and escaped to Tunisia to avoid the trial. The general secretary of Christian Democracy, Arnaldo Forlani, was arraigned in court and was found guilty of illegal party funding. The person in charge of Christian Democratic finances, together with his equivalent in the Socialist Party, was arrested. Business figures, too, were arrested and prosecuted. Within a period of a few weeks, all the old party organisations simply disappeared.

The only party to survive this storm was the Communist Party, though almost contemporaneously, the fall of the Berlin Wall and the collapse of Soviet communism forced it to undergo a fundamental internal revolution. Its name was changed from Partito Comunista Italiano to Partito Socialista Democratico, abandoning the traditional Communist symbolic framework that had been so much part of the political environment of its members and supporters. Its party structure and leadership also changed. Later, the party would change its name again, because of mergers with smaller parties from a Catholic tradition; its present incarnation is the Partito Democratico (PD). It was a shift both wide and deep, a sudden (though never violent) transition from the First, post-fascist, Republic to a Second Republic, the destruction of the previous political system creating a wholly new environment.

One of the consequences of this change was that voters could no longer find on their ballot paper the familiar symbols they were used to looking for and supporting: their 'own' party had disappeared from the ballot paper, and they were therefore open to new proposals. Silvio Berlusconi, a voracious consumer of survey research on political and cultural tendencies (Pilo, 1996), understood that there was a vacuum in the middle of the Italian political spectrum, a vacuum previously occupied by the parties supporting the centrist coalition (Democrazia Cristiana, Partito Socialista, Partito Repubblicano, Partito Socialdemocratico). Voters for these groups had become orphans. Berlusconi filled that vacuum.

What was new? First, from his debut in 1994, he understood that he needed to offer Italian citizens a completely new image of politics. His opinion polls told him that the public was angry at former politicians and former party organisations being so deeply involved in corrupt practices (even if many citizens had gained from them). As Alessandro Pizzorno has convincingly demonstrated, the success of the judges of Mani pulite in persecuting all those politicians who were involved in corruption was possible thanks to wide support from a very large part of public opinion in favour of action against the 'old' politics (Pizzorno, 1998). Berlusconi understood, thanks to his survey research, that there was a need for a clean break with the past.

And indeed, the symbolic framework within which he put his political proposal and his own political figure was new. He chose to present himself quite openly as the new politics opposed to the old that had been so widely rejected and discredited by a very large percentage of Italians (Abruzzese, 1994; Russo, 1994; Pilo, 1996). He adopted the tactic – familiar elsewhere, especially in the US – of competing as an outsider, running against a discredited system in which the insiders had been disgraced (Caniglia, 2000). He had success behind him: he had a very profitable business; he was the man who had renovated Italian television and who, together with his business success, could boast also great sporting success with AC Milan (which, by happy chance, won the 1994 national championship). Novelty, success and efficiency: these were the main symbolic elements of Berlusconi's political proposal (Dal Lago, 1994; Diamanti, 1994). This choice clearly won in the election of 1994, the first to be held after the Mani pulite scandals and the complete reshaping of the Italian political scene. In 2011, the symbolic dimension that Berlusconi proposed seventeen years ago remains almost unchanged.

Berlusconi between television, lifestyle politics, and commodification of politics

The symbolic and political imagery associated with Berlusconi is composed of three main elements: television, the commodification of politics, and lifestyle politics. In the following pages I shall try to explain these three components.

Television

The symbiosis between Silvio Berlusconi and television is not just a matter of ownership: it is something much more important and deeper, related to the gamut of dreams, symbols, images, values that represent the 'core business' of television culture. Berlusconi is not just the owner of television channels, he *is* television, in particular he is *commercial* television – with its culture, values, discourses, practices, aspirations. Again, I do not want to underestimate the importance of Berlusconi as owner of the major Italian commercial television corporation: but it is not sufficient to explain his political success.

If in the field of politics Berlusconi represents an important novelty, his innovations are even more important in the field of television itself. Commercial television in Italy is embodied in his figure, decisions, and activities. He founded the first, important commercial television, Canale5, at the end of the 1970s and progressively added the Italia1 and Rete4 networks, bought from defeated competitors. At the end of the 1980s he had completed the construction of his own television conglomerate, Fininvest (later transformed into Mediaset) and, essentially thanks to the political support of the Socialist party, he was able to transform the Italian television system from one of a public service monopoly into a mixed system, public and private – a substantially duopolistic situation, RAI and Fininvest, with no space for other possible competitors.

Just as the First Republic was replaced by the Second, with a new political system and new political assumptions, so the new commercial TV replaced the old public monopoly – not by taking over RAI (the public service broadcaster) but by forcing it to compete on Berlusconi's terms. Commercial television has radically changed the culture of Italy. The historian Antonio Gibelli writes that

> *until 1994 television had existed under the control of the State, interpreting the educational goals, the ideological codes and concerns of the Christian Democratic elite. Television had diffused a message marked by moderation, respect, instructive entertainment, paternalism and the cult of familiar intimacy. The transformation of television into a business aimed at making money has represented an enormous novelty . . . being a dreams factory, television suggested the possible interchangeability between the real and the virtual . . . . because, much more than cinema, television is marked by the blurring of differences in the unique dimension of everyday life.* (Gibelli, 2010: 15)

Neil Postman and others had already noted that entertainment was killing the old culture (Postman, 1985): but it was dramatically new and disruptive for the Italian cultural tradition, and for its once-stable political system.

Within a couple of decades – from being, in the first place, an educational tool subordinate to Catholic culture; then, in the 1970s, during the centre-left coalition governments, an instrument for the representation of political pluralism – Italian television was transformed into a profitable machine responding to the needs of commercial competition. In both private and public television, the demands of commercial competition were combined with attempts to use TV as an instrument to construct and to ensure political consensus.

An important part of Berlusconi's political success lies in his idea of television as a tool that dissolves the difference between real life and dreams, a tool of endless amusement, producing happiness and optimism. In an interview in 1977 he addressed the difference he saw between 'his' television and public service broadcasting – 'reality offers too many occasions that cause anxiety: mine will be an optimistic television'.[3] This is one of the basic formulae of his political success: he removes the barrier between virtual success (the imagery spread by his television) and being himself a successful person. Real and virtual overlap in his personal experience.

It is hard, even impossible, to produce hard figures for the effects of television in producing intimacy, aspirations, dreams and expectations. Nevertheless, there is indirect evidence that points towards a possible interpretation, and this will be illustrated in the following pages.

---

[3] Quoted in G. A. Stella, 'Passato presente di Silvio', *Il Corriere della Sera*, 29 Jan. 2011.

Lifestyle politics

The second main feature is what may be called lifestyle politics, an idea which first appeared in a paper by Lance Bennet. He argued that, because of changes taking place in the economic structure of the society, people were progressively retreating from public engagement, were abandoning any interest in public affairs, and getting more and more involved in 'smaller' issues, focused on private life and personal problems. These had become more important than community problems. Bennet writes 'the psychological energy (cathexis) people once devoted to the grand political projects of economic integration and nation building in industrial democracies is now increasingly directed toward personal projects of managing and expressing complex identities in a fragmented society' (1998: 755).

This tendency towards lifestyle politics was, and still is, determined by a process of atomisation of the society where personal identity is replacing collective identity as the main agent of engagement in the life of the community. There is a growing attention to all those post-materialist values that are a feature of modernity and that are linked to one's individual life and performance, having less regard to the group or the community to which each person belongs (Inglehart, 1997). The experiences that make up everyday life become progressively more important; they are the parameters through which public engagement is decided and evaluated: 'Individuals are simultaneously citizens, consumers, audiences, family members, workers and so forth. Politics is built on deep-seated cultural values and beliefs that are imbedded in the seemingly nonpolitical aspects of public and private life' (Delli Carpini and Williams, 2001).

The idea of lifestyle politics is used by many scholars to explain the shift from ideological and cultural considerations, and attitudes built in stable and organised visions of the society and its problems, towards more contingent problems of a specific nature linked to everyday life. The attention devoted to issues related to the environment, choices of consumption, and everyday behaviour assumes a political salience and they are interpreted as being indicators of a specific political choice. Rather than taking an active part in the life of political organisations, people demonstrate their political involvement by eating organic food, buying clothes produced by factories that do not employ minors, or paying more attention to products deriving from fair trade. 'Political consumerism' becomes a specific type of political engagement and choice (Micheletti, 2003; Shah and Strombcah, 2007).

Similarly, the concept of lifestyle politics may be a useful tool to explain why Berlusconi obtained, and still retains, such a large consensus among Italian citizens. The vote for Berlusconi may be interpreted as an explicit consensus about the way of life he embodies: it is a choice of consumption, a choice that goes in the opposite direction to most political consumerism. By voting Berlusconi, a large percentage of Italian citizens are choosing what seems to them to be the best way 'to promote personal lifestyle agendas of political and economic interest' (Bennet, 1998: 758). They are not interested in punishing factories which use products made by minors: instead, they want to vote for and to support someone who may improve their lifestyle and who personally embodies the level and way of life to which they aspire.

The idea of lifestyle politics implies that the separation between politics and other expressions of everyday life that existed decades ago, and that featured in and gave birth to the experience of mass parties, is no longer possible. When Lyotard in *La Condition postmoderne* talks about the end of those 'great' narratives of the previous century, and the impossibility of separating the different messages and experiences which each person continuously experiences today (Lyotard, 1979), he stresses the impossibility of isolating politics from consumption choices and from everyday aspirations, of separating politics from the time spent in coffee shops, at the stadium, with friends, on vacation.

The 'idea of lifestyle politics' embodies the impossibility of this separation: on one side, following Bennet and others, 'consumerism' may become political; but one can also say that a political choice for Berlusconi, may, in the same way, embody a complete framework of aspirations deeply rooted in everyday life. As Beppe Severgnini, a leading Italian journalist, has convincingly demonstrated, Berlusconi is the 'belly of the Italians'. He has transferred the dreams, the aspirations of many Italian citizens into a political programme and a political-symbolic apparatus. 'It is in the bar, not in research institutes, that elections are won. The only one who doesn't understand this is Massimo D'Alema'[4] (Severgnini, 2010: 25).

This overlap between everyday life and politics is pushed even further by the language that Berlusconi uses. His words and his statements do not have anything in common with previous political experience in Italy, where the language used was formal, stilted and separate from everyday experience. He uses phrases and expressions that every Italian citizen uses

---

[4] Massimo D'Alema is one of the most important leaders of the present Partito Democratico. He was the leader of the Communist party and Prime Minister and Minister for Foreign Affairs. He established an important leftist think-tank: Italiani/europei.

continuously at home, the expressions Italians use to address relatives, friends, parents.

Stephen Coleman has a nice comparison between those who live in the Big Brother house, and those who live in the House of Commons: 'popular culture celebrates self-presentation through music, slang, travel, gadgets or fashion. The political elite is not only often impervious to such trends, but dismisses them with condescension or contempt' (Coleman, 2003: 56). Berlusconi seems to be able to connect the two houses: he has established a new political culture, rooted in the everyday experience of those who live in the House of Big Brother – and similar houses.

Commodification of politics

The expression 'commodification of politics' suggests the overlap between politics and consumption – in the sense that a political choice may also imply a world of commercial values, imagery, and commodities, i.e. it is deeply rooted in consumption. The values of the market are becoming the values of politics: the voter supports a specific party or a politician, in this case, Berlusconi, as his figure identifies the values the voter aspires to possess. In their recent book on *The Internet and Democratic Citizenship*, Coleman and Blumler confirm this tendency: 'in their approach to politics, citizens have become more like consumers (instrumental, oriented to immediate gratifications and potentially fickle) than believers' (2009: 46). This is another confirmation of some kind of universal tendency.

What are these values? Wealth, consumption, holidays, beautiful and elegant men and women, fun, popular music (Berlusconi himself is an experienced singer,[5] and is always accompanied by his personal musician, Mariano D'Apicella), dancing, jokes (Berlusconi tells jokes on every possible occasion).

This is a dramatic shift from the old, traditional values of politics as they were experienced for much of the post-war period: the values of equality, solidarity, of welfare state, of left and right, of progressivism opposed to conservatism – all of these are losing importance. Policy issues play an apparently minor role in the new political language. Berlusconi doesn't talk the usual language of politics, doesn't talk much about policy issues: instead, he prefers to tell jokes to involve and motivate people. Amusement comes first, and amusement is inextricably linked to wealth: during a public meeting, when asked by a pretty young girl how to find a

---

[5] In his youth Berlusconi used to earn money singing on cruise boats.

job, Berlusconi suggested she look for a possible rich husband – better, his own son.[6]

Another very important indicator of commodification of politics is related to the history and the structure itself of the party, Forza Italia, that Berlusconi established. At the end of 1993 and the beginning of 1994 Berlusconi transferred a large part of the personnel of his television company into the newly established party. Many officials from Fininvest and Publitalia (Berlusconi's advertising company) were asked to move into the organisation of the party, and even today some of the important members of the Partito della Libertà originally worked for these companies (Poli, 2001). The personal experiences of Marcello Dell'Utri and Gianni Pilo are of particular interest: Marcello Dell'Utri, presently a member of parliament (and accused of involvement with the mafia), was chairman of Publitalia, and one of the main founders of Forza Italia, together with Silvio Berlusconi and Giuliano Urbani. Gianni Pilo was the head of marketing for Fininvest when he was asked by Berlusconi to establish a new survey research company in charge of all the opinion polls that helped give birth to Forza Italia. A considerable part of the entrepreneurial culture that ensured the success of the television conglomerate, Fininvest, over its competitors was moved into Forza Italia and permeated the political choices and activities of this new established party.

Berlusconeries

By the term 'Berlusconeries' I refer to those actions and statements by Berlusconi that, for many both in Italy and abroad, sound – when compared to the traditional language of politics – strange and exotic, often interpreted as gaffes and mistakes, or as evidence of a lack of experience in politics. Berlusconeries can be placed within the field of audience democracy: through their use, the Prime Minister is talking directly to his own audience, proposing a way of life and the images that he knows his audience likes. Berlusconeries are deeply rooted in the commodification of politics as the values, dreams, images they put on stage are those of consumption and market.

The very body of Berlusconi has become a site of political, as well as erotic, power. Filippo Ceccarelli, a journalist for *La Repubblica*, comments:

---

[6] Quoted in Severgnini (2010: 121).

To be sure: no leader before had put his body at the very centre of the political narration, giving his public continuous news on food, diet, jogging, biological age, hours of sleeping, lost and earned kilos, miles of flight, numbers of meetings, miraculous elixirs, medical herbs at his Villa Certosa,[7] sexual dreams and hints on other miraculous medicines . . . in a suggestive and sensual abundance that restarts symbolic discourses around the body of the king, with all the magic resources of power and that Berlusconi is able to transfer into today's language.[8]

Berlusconi devotes great attention to his body and appearance, and cares greatly about looking elegant: he constantly criticises his party members, deputies and senators for not being elegant enough. Several scholars have written about Berlusconi's physical aspect, and how his body is able to carry many of the features of audience democracy in its commodified version (see Belpoliti, 2009). Severgnini's book is full of nice anecdotes about the care he lavishes on his body and his public appearance (Severgnini, 2010).

Let me illustrate some Berlusconeries.

16 August 2004: Berlusconi walks around the tiny streets of Porto Rotondo, a luxurious resort in Sardinia where he owns a vast mansion, Villa La Certosa, the subject of many news stories and much criticism. He wears a showy bandana, probably because he has just had a hair transplant – one of the most obvious ways in which he seeks to maintain an air of relative youth. He is walking about with Cherie and Tony Blair, recently arrived to visit him in this golden resort. Porto Rotondo, with nearby Porto Cervo, are where celebrities, movie stars and young, brilliant entrepreneurs spend their vacations and meet other important and wealthy people. These places are world famous for their discos and nightclubs, the most noted of which is, not by chance, named The Billionaire. All who want to enter show business have to spend at least one week in one of these resorts: the gossip weeklies will cover their adventures and their love affairs.

Much more than in other months, in August these places are crowded with thousands of people while Berlusconi takes a walk with his guests. As in the past centuries, when the King would decide to drive in a horse and carriage through the streets outside his castle to show the symbols of his

[7] Villa La Certosa is Berlusconi's luxurious home in Sardinia.
[8] F. Ceccarelli 'Lifting, sciataglie, pacemaker: Ecco la biopolitica del Cavaliere', *La Repubblica*, 8 June 2008.

power, so Berlusconi decides that it is time to leave his luxurious residence and to plunge into the midst of the vacation crowd. Unlike a king, though, his symbols are not the obvious ones: he decides to look as far as possible like a common man, albeit with a wealthy lifestyle. The bandana he wears is what young, fashionable people often wear when they are enjoying life. It is not, for all that, the common headgear of ordinary people: it is headgear worn by those who want to indicate an unconventional approach to life. It suggests days and nights spent on the beach playing music and having fun. It is used in TV commercials promoting products for young, good-looking people. To complete his uniform, Berlusconi wears white trousers and a white shirt – again, a sign of freedom, vacation time, summertime.

The entire symbolic framework of Berlusconi's appearance in the streets of Porto Rotondo is the strongest possible indicator of the commodification of politics, centuries away from traditional Italian political settings, when no politician would think of appearing in public dressed in such a way. The dark suit is the conventional uniform of Italian – and many other – politicians. In the pictures of Berlusconi that circulate around the world, there is no symbolic reference to social solidarity, economic equity, the welfare state on the one hand, or an attachment to national identity and security on the other. His appearance in public has no reference to the most traditional symbolic construction of political debate, its issues, its seriousness and separation from everyday life.

The difference from the past is even more striking if we consider how far this image is from that of the former leaders of Italian politics. Arnaldo Forlani, a leader of the Christian Democrats, was never seen smiling, was slow in speech, invariably serious, giving no sign of emotional involvement; Aldo Moro, killed by the Red Brigades, embodied the image of religious asceticism and seriousness; and Enrico Berlinguer, the Communist leader, was known for his support for a political programme based on 'austerity'. These were the Italian versions of Dik Pels's already-quoted 'reigning LabLib elite' (Pels, 2003: 42).

Another example. On 1 July 2003 Silvio Berlusconi attended the European Parliament in Strasbourg where, in a debate, the leader of the German SPD delegation, Martin Schulz, accused him of a conflict of interests. Berlusconi replied: 'Mr Schulz, in Italy there is a film director who is preparing a movie on concentration camps. I will suggest to him that he consider you for the role of the German Kapò.'[9] The storm of

---

[9] 'Il duello verbale Schulz–Berlusconi', *La Repubblica*, 2 July 2003.

criticism which followed, from left and right, was not only political, but a matter of propriety: to call someone a kapò, or a guard in a concentration camp, is far from the tone of the traditional political debate. Newspapers in Italy and throughout the world were united in accusing him of using outrageous language, of having revived a tragic past better forgotten. Yet what Berlusconi put on the public stage was a stereotype drawn from the images and TV programmes which still play and replay the Nazi past – and which means that the image of the German kapò is diffused through everyday Italian, and world, culture: as elsewhere, the words and expressions drawn from Nazism are used to express disapproval, and as common insults. A few years earlier, in his 1993 Oscar-winning movie *La vita è bella* ('Life is Beautiful') Roberto Benigni had splendidly depicted the figure of a German kapò and his rude language.

Italy's Prime Minister Silvio Berlusconi joins AC Milan with the Champions League trophy after they defeated Liverpool in the final soccer match in Athens, May 23, 2007. REUTERS/Phil Noble

And finally, sport. Sport has always been an important part of Berlusconi's programme from the moment he decided to enter the political arena. The very name of the party he established, Forza Italia, is what football fans shout when the national team is playing (Dal Lago, 1994; Diamanti, 1994).

Probably the most striking occasion during which Berlusconi showed how deeply his public and political personality is embodied in sport took place on 22 February 2002: during one of the most successful shows on RAI completely devoted to sport news *La Domenica Sportiva*, he phoned the anchorman and talked on air for almost twenty minutes. His point was a simple one: AC Milan (the team he owns) should play with two players forward, and not just with one – as Milan's coach, Carlo Ancellotti, preferred. Berlusconi argued at length on this point, saying that what counts in sport is the 'the philosophy of spectacle'. This, he said, is more important than merely winning the game: if one only seeks to win, the spectators may be offered a very boring match. The long phone call, broadcast live, gave rise to a lot of criticism. The then president of RAI's board of directors, Lucia Annunziata, called the anchorman once Berlusconi had finished, and criticised Berlusconi for 'his inappropriate occupation of airtime': her call was also broadcast live. Other calls followed, making the same point: Berlusconi was invading the field of sport to address a large audience shortly before an election campaign.

Football is much of life – at least, male life – in Italy. It occupies most of the many newspapers and broadcasts dedicated to sport. It is what Italians discuss when they go to the bar, when they sit in open-air cafés.

As Severgnini reminds us, 'it is in the bar that elections are won'. By calling the *Domenica Sportiva* anchorman, Berlusconi becomes part of the everyday life of Italian citizens: 'I'm just like you are'; 'I like to talk about the same topics you like'. His intervention was a vivid example of lifestyle politics, of the overlap between everyday life and politics. No need for obscure, difficult, ambiguous topics – the stuff of which real politics is made and which governments must resolve, and are expected, in some form, to lay before their citizens for their judgement. Instead he speaks to people in a way which leads them to think 'today, in the political arena, there is someone like me; I can trust this person; I share the same feelings'.

Berlusconeries don't end here. The list is very long: showing his Latin lover side, Berlusconi confesses that he has been trying to seduce the Finnish Prime Minister so that she will accept the Italian city of Parma being nominated the seat of the European food authority. TV viewers all around the world have seen Berlusconi playing hide and seek with Angela Merkel while both were en route to a meeting of G8 leaders; and there is a wonderful picture of Berlusconi looking entranced at the beauty of Michelle Obama – while her husband looks on with an apparently worried expression. It is a perfect image of the typical Italian man; what Italian man, after all, would not react in a similar way when confronted with a beautiful woman?

Italy's Prime Minister Silvio Berlusconi (L) greets U.S. President Barack Obama and first lady Michelle Obama as they arrive at the Phipps Conservatory for an opening reception and working dinner for heads of delegation at the G20 Summit in Pittsburgh, Pennsylvania, September 24, 2009. REUTERS/Jim Young

These are not gaffes. Instead, these episodes demonstrate that Berlusconi is perfectly aware of the changed character of politics. He knows that he is a performer before an audience; to gain and to maintain the trust of these who are watching him he has chosen to embody the fantasies of ordinary people. To these people, he offers the dream of success in business and in sport, a wealthy and good life. To make this dream seem even more possible, he talks and behaves as the people he addresses do.

Is this just a matter of a sophisticated communication strategy? I think that this interpretation, too, would be wrong. Berlusconi is changing the nature of politics, replacing its previous character with a new one. Everyday life and consumption are becoming the driving characters of his political image.

3. Berlusconi: Universal Tendencies and National Identity

Does an Italian case exist?

At this point, one major question has to be asked: are the transformations implied in Berlusconi's political adventure related only to the Italian case? Or do they have some sort of universal applicability? I would respond positively to both questions: there are many Berlusconis around the world; yet still, the figure of the present Italian Prime Minister has to be understood and interpreted in relationship to the specific Italian political landscape and to its political culture. I have already highlighted the observations of many scholars, both in political science and in media studies, on the weakening role of mass parties and the increasing role of mass media; the process of personalisation and presidentialisation; the increasingly frequent overlap between popular culture and politics. The tendency towards atomisation that both commodification of politics and lifestyle politics encourage is a more or less universal one which can be observed in many democratic countries. Berlusconi embodies all these changes within a set of national characteristics that may make these features even more evident and dramatic: and this in turn must be related to the low level of civic culture and the strong dependency on television that are a feature of Italy today. This chapter will deal with these two questions.

When, in different parts of the world, I give presentations on Berlusconi following the interpretive schema suggested in this essay, the most common comment from people in established democracies is 'this could never happen in my country'. But the comments from people in transitional or new democracies are very different: usually some variant of 'there are many Berlusconis in my country'. The first comment may or may not be true: certainly, this comment implies some sort of national character that may explain the Berlusconi case and his very 'Italian nature'. And, at the same time, the comment 'there are many Berlusconis in my country' underlines a set of conditions that may be found in other countries as well – even settled, democratic ones.

The question could be reversed: 'how is it possible that this happens in Italy?' Many observers comment on the exceptionality of the Italian case. Insofar as it exists, it is to be found, I believe, in two main characteristics of Italian identity: the low level of civic culture and the strong dependence on television by a large part of Italian population. These two features are so closely connected with each other that the discussion of one implies frequent cross-reference to the other. That these features may be found in other countries accounts for the frequency of the comment: 'there are many Berlusconis in my country'. And indeed, if on one side the Berlusconi case illustrates tendencies that, at different levels and with different intensity, have some universal character, nevertheless it has to be said that 'other Berlusconis' may more easily appear in those countries that present those features that seem to characterise the Italian cultural, social, and political context: a mass media system organised around the main role of television and a very pronounced inclination towards particularism, together with what Max Weber would define as a low level of rational-legal authority, that is, the absence (or weakness) of a system of rules having universal character.

We have seen that in Italy there was an almost complete disappearance of the previous party system in 1992 and 1993, leaving a political vacuum that Berlusconi was able to fill. Berlusconi was able to build successful political alliances with other parties, and in particular with Lega Nord. Undoubtedly, he commands enormous wealth and resources, including communication resources. His insistence on anti-communism revives the old and deep fracture between 'reds' and 'whites' that was a feature of Italy during the First Republic, which still resonates with many on left and right.

But above all, there is no doubt that Berlusconi, with his closest collaborators, has been able to put together a political programme that meets the demands of a large number of Italian voters. I want to stress this point. He was able to address popular aspirations in 1994 when he decided to enter the political arena – and he is still able to meet these expectations today. The novelty lies in the fact that most of these expectations are not traditional 'political' expectations: these he has not, in general, addressed successfully. He successfully addressed issues, topics, perceptions, emotions that were produced by the mass media system. Moreover, we should remember that the majority of Italian citizens was, and still is, very disappointed with traditional politics – a disappointment which is in line with that in other Western democracies (Norris, 2011).

I see three main changes in the field of cultural consumption that may be useful in explaining the Berlusconi case, and how far it is in line with that of other leaders:

- an increase in the circulation of information and opportunities, and the ability to get news from many, often contrasting, sources;
- the overlapping of political knowledge with many other everyday and mediated experiences;
- an increasing attitude towards forms of consumption that prefigures the passive role of spectator in front of many different performances.

The pluralisation of sources of information

Before the arrival of television and the dramatic increase in most of the different forms of cultural consumption, politics was a symbolic environment well separated from everyday life. There were moments when (mostly) men used to go to party branches and discuss political matters; there were moments in which both men and women joined political rallies and demonstrations; there were moments of mobilisation, of grass-roots propaganda, of electioneering. There were other, less organised moments when politics was discussed: but these were the times in life specifically devoted to political discussions and activities. Very often, the election campaign was the only significant occasion on which political matters were brought before men and women who – with the obvious exception of those who had some kind of stable political commitment – would largely ignore them.

The development of the mass media, and television in particular, has dramatically changed this. First of all, the number of occasions to learn about politics and politicians has increased enormously. TV news, talk shows, and entertainment programmes are crowded with politicians: there is no need to leave the house to watch and hear political interviews, speeches, and arguments. Politics is presented to citizens by newspapers, TV, radio, and the internet. And it is presented together with thousands of other social and symbolic experiences with which it is combined. The main consequence is that political parties have lost the monopoly (or the quasi-monopoly) of political information and analysis: in Italy, this is particularly marked, because parties have always played a very large role as agencies of political socialisation. Data from different sources are very clear about this shift.

Table 1. How do you get news about the election campaign? (%)
   Source: Itanes 2008

Radio	35.2
Television	81.1
Newspapers	61.1
Meetings, demonstrations, etc	12.9
Internet	17.5

In the 2008 election campaign, 81% of the voters got news from the television and only 12.9% actively participated in some political events. This latter figure is not, in fact, low, compared to other European countries: data from World Values Survey 2005–8 demonstrate that in Europe, Italy comes fourth after Switzerland, Norway and the Netherlands in active involvement with political parties that emerges when people take part in demonstrations and meetings (www.worldvaluessurvey.org). But a comparison between cultural consumption in Italy and other Western democracies highlights an important difference: Italy has, relatively speaking, a low level of print press circulation and a high level of television consumption.

In *Comparing Media Systems* (Hallin and Mancini, 2004) we noted that the countries of the Mediterranean or part of the polarised/pluralist model (including Italy) are marked by high television consumption and low print press circulation. A recent article by Adam Shehata and Jesper Strömbäck is relevant here. The two authors carried out a study on the different attitudes to media consumption in some of the major Western democracies. In Figures 1 and 2, Italy, together with all the other Mediterranean countries, is 'clustered in the lower right corner, reflecting their lower levels of newspaper-centrism' (Shehata and Strömbäck, 2011: 118). These figures offer a graphic representation of the data contained in another more complete table (Table 2) that clearly confirm the low level of print press circulation and the higher TV consumption in Italy. This 'television centrism' points to an at least partial explanation of Berlusconi's success in attracting the attention, and the votes, of large numbers of Italians.

Table 2. Levels of newspaper reading and television viewing in Europe

	Average time spent watching television (ESS data)[a]	Average time spent reading newspapers (ESS data)[b]	Average television viewing per person (minutes/day 2004)[c]	Average newspaper circulation per 1,000 adults (2004)[d]
Austria	3.78	1.70	156	372
Belgium	4.28	1.09	193	173
Switzerland	3.25	1.66	166	398
Germany	4.32	1.52	210	313
Denmark	4.28	1.42	161	301
Spain	4.24	0.91	218	123
Finland	3.91	1.77	167	522
France	4.35	1.06	204	160
United Kingdom	5.06	1.61	222	332
Greece	5.06	0.70	244	68
Ireland	4.58	2.06	177	234
Italy	4.62	1.20	240	115
Netherlands	4.51	1.57	192	303
Norway	3.90	1.95	156	651
Portugal	4.16	0.97	214	69
Sweden	3.75	1.68	151	489

a. Mean scores of the general television viewing scale ranging from 0 (no time at all) to 7 (more than 3 hours). Source: European Social Survey (2008) cumulative data, rounds 1–3.

b. Mean scores of the general newspaper reading scale ranging from 0 (no time at all) to 7 (more than 3 hours). Source: European Social Survey (2008) cumulative data, rounds 1–3.

c. **Source:** European Audiovisual Observatory (2009).

d. **Source:** World Association of Newspapers (2005).

Both in terms of time spent reading newspapers/watching television and print press circulation, the two different sources demonstrate that Italy is well behind most of Western democracies in term of 'written culture'. It seems, instead, to be more inclined towards a visual culture.

Other comparative data (Censis and Ucsi, 2006) confirm the Shehata and Strömbäck analysis. In Italy, as in most of the Mediterranean or polarised/pluralist model countries, there has long been a rooted tradition of an elite press, addressed essentially to an educated readership already socialised to political life. The absence of a popular daily press increases the importance of television as the main source both for soft and hard news, and for entertainment.

Figure 1. Newspaper/television-centrism in Europe

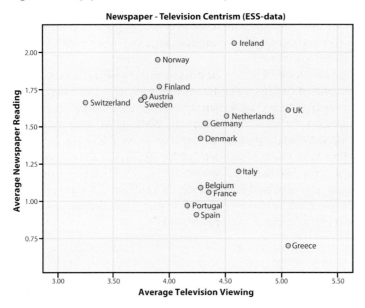

Figure 2. Newspaper/television-centrism in Europe

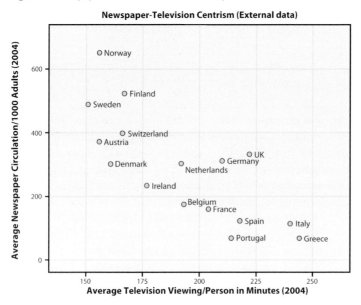

These data tell us that a large part of Italian citizens, a larger percentage than in other Western democracies, depends on television for their everyday information. And within this structural dependency there is one figure, Silvio Berlusconi, who occupies a large part of television output, who himself *is* 'television'.

If we go deeper into the available data, we discover that within the more general television centrism, Berlusconi voters are even more dependent on television than the average Italian citizens. Different indicators support this conclusion: Table 3 shows that, in 2008, those who voted for Berlusconi were somewhat more dependent on television for their information than those who voted for his opponent, Walter Veltroni (41.4% against 36.3%). Table 3 demonstrates also that the level of political participation is somewhat higher among the centre-leftist voters: 8.1% of those who voted for Veltroni took an active part in the election campaign, against 6% of those who voted for Berlusconi.

Table 3. From which source voters of Popolo della Libertà (Berlusconi) and Partito Democratico (Veltroni) get news about the campaign (%) (more than one answer possible)
Source: Itanes 2008

		Radio	Television	Newspapers	Meetings, demonstrations, etc.	Internet	Total
Partito Democratico (Veltroni)	Count	260	542	446	121	122	1491
	%	17.4	36.4	29.9	8.1	8.2	100
Popolo della Libertà (Berlusconi)	Count	205	481	336	70	69	1161
	%	17.7	41.4	28.9	6	5.9	100
Other voters	Count	164	321	249	58	90	882
	%	18.6	36.4	28.2	6.6	10.2	100
No answer	Count	243	617	430	57	86	1433
	%	17	43.1	30	4	6	100

Other studies by Itanes (Italian National Election Studies) on Italian elections have demonstrated that women, and particularly housewives, are Berlusconi's most loyal voters. The authors of the study on the 2008 political elections write that the votes for PdL, and for the centre-right in general, come from 'housewives, half of whom had voted for PdL; if the other parties on the centre-right are added to this list, the result is that almost 70% of women have voted for centre-right' (Maraffi, 2008).[10] Table 4 shows the data supporting this conclusion.

Table 4. Women voters by occupation (%)
   Source: Itanes 2008

	PD	PDL	OTHERS	TOTAL	(N)
Retired people	38.9	40.0	21.1	100.0	180
Housewives	22.9	49.0	28.1	100.0	210
Students	31.0	22.5	46.5	100.0	71
Working women	37.2	35.7	27.1	100.0	258
Total	31.7	40.9	27.4	100.0	772

Itanes data demonstrate also that women voting for Berlusconi are among the largest television consumers in Italy. Table 5 shows data from another Itanes research on political elections in 2001 and demonstrates how, of the four major parties, 36.6% of women vote for Berlusconi's Forza Italia and 42.3% of those who watch television for more than three hours a day vote for the present Italian Prime Minister.

Table 5. Women voters by time spent in front of TV (%)
   Source: Itanes 2001

	An*	FI*	Margherita*	Ds*
From 1 to 2 hours	8.1	31.6	17.4	22.3
From 2 to 3 hours	8.8	35.4	15.7	21.4
More than 3	11.5	42.3	10.7	17.8
Total	9.5	36.6	14.5	20.4

* These political parties are now under different names
An: Alleanza Nazionale; FI: Forza Italia; DS: Democratici della Sinistra

Other data tend to confirm the remark by Norberto Bobbio at the beginning of this essay, that 'it is not Berlusconi who wins, it is the society that his mass media organizations have created that wins'. There is a

---

[10] In 2008 elections the centre-right coalition was composed of Popolo della Libertà (PdL), Lega, Destra. Udc was not part of the centre-right coalition but it is a centre-right party.

marked and apparently stable connection between Berlusconi voters and his television networks' viewers. Indeed, by knowing how many citizens watch either Canale5 or Rete4 or Italia1 (the Mediaset channels), it is possible to predict an electoral outcome. In the 2008 Itanes study the authors write that 'the importance of television is associated with one of the major characteristics of the election in the Second Republic: the alignment between electoral choices and TV consumption' (Legnante and Sani, 2008).

Table 6. TV news consumption by vote (%)
    Source: Itanes 2008

	PD	PDL	Other voters	Total	(N)
Rai1	33.3	24.2	42.4	100.0	702
Rai2	32.1	18.5	49.5	100.0	81
Rai3	44.4	9.1	46.4	100.0	297
Canale5	10.1	50.9	39.1	100.0	525
Italia1	11.7	39.4	49.0	100.0	94
Rete4	6.8	59.3	33.9	100.0	59
La7	32.0	14.0	54.0	100.0	50
Others	22.3	19.4	58.3	100.0	139

Of those who watch Canale5 (the major Mediaset channel) 50.9% vote for the PdL, while only 10.1% vote for the major competing party, the PD. On the opposite side, 44.4% of those who watch RAI3 (the traditionally leftist public channel) vote PD while only 9.1% vote PdL. These data confirm the results of several previous studies (Itanes, 2001, 2006) and stress the high level of political parallelism existing in the Italian public sphere; there is a very strong correlation between the political dimension of the media message and the electoral choices of its receivers/users. Leftist channels are consumed by leftist people and the rightist channel by rightist voters. This would appear not to encourage the sharing of a field of common interests and values; instead it pushes the society towards a polarisation of political options and affiliations – and these, till recently, have helped make possible the recurring victories of the centre-right.

Two further comments on the data on television consumption. First, Italian citizens are more dependent on television in general than citizens of the other Western democracies – and it appears at least likely that this high level of television consumption encourages some sort of symbiosis between the man who owns such an important part of Italian television system and a large percentage of the citizens of this country. Television content fits perfectly into the Berlusconeries we have discussed. Visual discourse does not facilitate reflection and deep investigation of the broadcast topics: on the contrary it is more inclined towards simplification, emotionality, weak rationality, and visual involvement (Sartori, 2000). Consumerism seems to embody perfectly these features.

Secondly, there seems to be an even stricter correlation between the vote for Forza Italia/PdL and the consumption of Berlusconi's channels. On the one hand, this may indicate that there is a very strong symbiosis between the content of commercial television (better than public service television) and the vote for the centre-right parties. Commercial television, more than public service broadcasting, is permeated by consumption, entertainment, and a 'soft' culture. On the other hand we may assume that Mediaset channels influence voting intentions more directly, with news and content biased in favour of the owner of these channels.

Several years ago Pierpaolo Pasolini, the famous movie director, writer and journalist, discussed the 'anthropological' mutation produced by television (Pasolini, 1975). He put forward the idea that twenty years of television had changed Italian people more than twenty years of fascism. Even more recently, Ernesto Galli Della Loggia, a well-known historian and commentator for *Il Corriere della Sera*, not a leftist, has suggested a very similar thesis underlining how

> the life of people who live in this country, the framework of their emotions and passions is subtly, but forever, distorted, manipulated and then rearranged together in a new way by television . . . it is in the air time devoted to television entertainment that the destructive manipulation of the 'Italian anthropology' takes place . . . [T]elevision mud has replaced the cultural hegemony over the Italian people that its ruling elites are no longer able to exercise.[11]

Galli della Loggia ends his article by stressing how Berlusconi is not to be blamed for this anthropological mutation, since commercial television exists in many other countries and has not produced such a devastating mutation. If television has had such a devastating effect on society, it is because of Italian history itself, he concludes.

To anticipate the criticism: there are no data that support, explicitly and directly, this thesis. I think that it would be impossible to find evidence demonstrating conclusively that Italian citizens vote for Berlusconi

[11] E. Galli della Loggia, 'Se la televisione si sostituisce alle élite: Come cambia l'antropologia italiana', *Il Corriere della Sera*, 20 Feb. 2011.

because they watch a lot of television and a specific sort of television.[12] At the same time it seems to me that there are data that point to a more indirect correlation between the vote for Berlusconi and the level of television consumption, between the vote for Berlusconi and the consumption of specific kinds of broadcasting. This kind of media consumption may facilitate the introduction of political choice within a framework of values and imagery that are directly related to commodification and everyday life.

Overlapping discourses and the disappearing specificity of politics

The increasing possibility of access to a variety of communication sources and the major role played by television as a socialisation agency (especially in the Italian case), makes it impossible for politics to survive as a field separated from the other fields, among which politics itself is placed when it is represented in television and through television.

Most of the time, politics is mixed with a number of other different social discourses: with different subjects of the news, with entertainment, music, and movies. Politics has lost its 'sacredness', its right to separation from other social experiences. Lyotard's observation on the impossibility of separating the different messages and narrations to which each single person is exposed everyday is above all the case in the act of viewing TV. The 'great' narrative of politics (to use Lyotard's words again), with its values, aspirations, and dreams, its large and often utopian ideals that addressed and influenced the political struggle and the formation of mass parties during the last century, today mixes with images of singers, dancers, and good-looking young men and women in the various national Big Brother houses, or with movie stars promoting, as Bobbio put it, ' this or that product'.

Here, the data do demonstrate that a correlation exists between the consumption of this kind of television broadcasting and electoral choice. There is a slight but nevertheless evident preference of right-wing voters for television entertainment, movies, and infotainment (Figure 3). These are the genres where television imagery is essentially constructed: here the values of success, beauty, consumption, as well as the representation of everyday life, play the leading role. A survey conducted in Umbria during local elections demonstrates that those who vote for the centre-right

---

[12] In an article, the sociologist Luca Ricolfi demonstrated the strict correlation existing during the 1994 election campaign between the consumption of Fininvest channels and the vote for Forza Italia (Ricolfi, 1994).

candidate watch more entertainment, movies, and infotainment than centre-left voters, while those who vote for the centre-left coalition are more interested in hard news and current affairs programmes. I am very well aware of the fact that these are just partial data that nevertheless, all together, contribute to establish a coherent interpretive framework of the attitudes of Italian voters.

Figure 3. Preferred programmes by centre-right/centre-left voters during 2010 local elections in Umbria

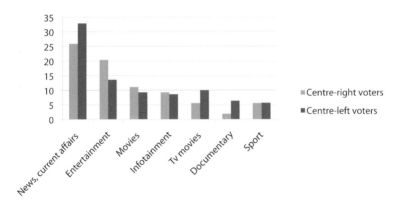

Figure 4 shows the existence of a strong correlation between centre-right voters and the very well-known TV programme *Big Brother*, a programme generally thought of as embodying the values of commodification and lifestyle politics. *Big Brother* blurs the boundaries between a virtual and a real experience: as the presenter endlessly repeats, the main stage is a 'real' house, which the participants enter dreaming of a successful future as movie/television star; they aim at entering the world of spectacle – and sometimes succeed. But they are also ordinary people, for whom, as Coleman has noted, the Big Brother house is more meaningful than the Houses of Parliament. The movie *Videocracy*[13] has vividly demonstrated the symbiosis existing between those of centre-right views and this kind of programme.

---

[13] *Videocracy* by the Italian/Swedish director Erik Gandini presents a highly critical version of the story of Berlusconi and his television empire.

Figure 4. Appreciation of *Big Brother* by voting intention

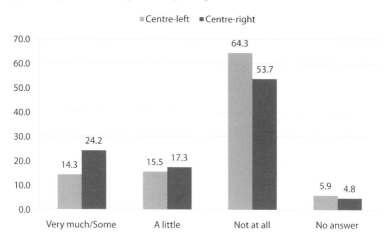

Who wants to be a Millionaire? is a programme which boldly announces its aim in its title. In this case, 12% of centre-right voters like it, against 4.2% of centre left voters; 33.5% of centre-left voters dislike it, against 21.6% of centre right voters (Figure 5). (Remember: the name of nightclub in Porto Rotondo is The Billionaire.)

Figure 5. How much do you like *Chi vuol essere milionario* by vote

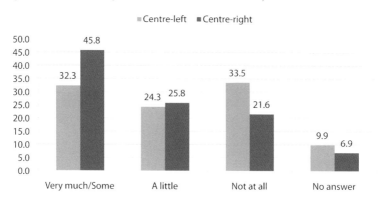

As Manin (together with many others) has suggested, in today's politics, citizens are mainly spectators. In Table 1 we saw that relatively few citizens are active in political life, taking little or no part in meetings, discussion, party activities, and so on. Some 12.9% of Italian citizens had this active role during the 2008 political elections – and while this is relatively high in European terms, it is a sharp fall from much higher levels of participation in a country whose parties were among the strongest, most active, and most numerous in the democratic world. Thus a slight but important difference emerges between centre-left and centre-right voters: the latter have a less active role in politics. They are more spectators than active participants in political life: it seems that the idea of audience democracy is more linked to the centre-right voters than to the centre-left.

How Berlusconi fits into national identity

Is what had seemed, until recently (spring 2011), to be a long honeymoon between Berlusconi and most Italian citizens simply a matter of television consumption? How is it that the commodification of politics – which Berlusconi holds out to Italian citizens, so closely tied to the values and to the most stereotyped imagery of success and money – is still so appealing? Can the populist display of everyday life which the Italian Prime Minister so enthusiastically and constantly presents to his country influence Italian politics so deeply, overcoming its traditional, symbolic and cultural structures? Has this to do with some Italian uniqueness? Why do so many British and German people say that Berlusconi would never be possible in their country? And yet why, on the contrary, do there seem to be so many Berlusconis in the new democracies of Central and Eastern Europe and beyond? Why do many observers talk of the Hungarian Prime Minister, Victor Orban, as a possible Berlusconi emulator? Here some other Italian uniqueness plays some role in explaining the Berlusconi success.

Indeed, in the world constructed by Berlusconi, universal rules on the new forms of politics found in different degrees of intensity in many different countries mix together with specific features of Italian national identity. Berlusconi embodies many of the very well-established aspects of Italian culture: he embodies some of worst parts of that identity. Berlusconi would not see himself in that light, but he does recognise his role as an aspirational figure, asking rhetorically on one occasion 'Why do my fellow citizens like me so much? Because the largest part of Italians would, fundamentally, wish to be like me.'[14] And what he seems to stand for, and what the results from the survey research I discuss below point out, is a high level of individualism, slight attention to common good, an extreme interest in success and money, and a very low level of respect for the rules. These are some of the features that make up the Italian national identity (at least they make up a large part of it) and that, beyond other general tendencies that it is possible to observe in many other parts of the world, may explain the possible uniqueness of the Berlusconi case. Nevertheless, as already said, other Berlusconis in other parts of the world may be explained by the presence of the same (or similar) features.

In a recent issue of the leftist journal *Reset*, the sociologist Alessandro Ferrara writes, provocatively:

> *Italy is a corrupt country, much more corrupt than any other similar country – and its political elite perfectly reflects this national character. We should look at very distant examples, where a relationship with democracy is much weaker, such as the Russia of the oligarchs, to find something similar. Berlusconi is the leader who is closer to such a moral decay.* (Ferrara, 2011: 33)

Discussions about Berlusconi's conflict of interests, his alleged possible connections with the mafia, and assumptions that many of his activities are corrupt, are continuous subjects of newspaper articles and books (Ginsborg, 2004). Beppe Severgnini writes: 'thanks to his private success, Berlusconi has constructed his political success on distrust towards everything that is the public and shared property of the community, on intolerance towards rules, and on the satisfaction to be found in finding private solutions to all collective problems' (Severgini, 2010: 48).

Itanes data from 2006 study seem to confirm Severgnini's observation: 'while centre-left voters give more importance to the values of universalism and solidarity, centre-right voters place greater weight on the contrasting values of success and power' (Catellani and Milesi, 2006: 154).

---

[14] Quoted in Severgnini (2010: 164).

Table 7. Importance given by Italian voters to specific values in 2006 political elections (average scale: from 5 = max agreement to 0 = no agreement at all)
Source: Itanes 2006

	Forza Italia voters	Ulivo voters
Success, being successful	2.06	1.95
Being ambitious	1.87	1.63
Power, being in power	1.43	1.16
Being rich	1.22	0.95
Same opportunities for all	2.32	2.53
Being tolerant	2.17	2.34
Kindness, helping people	2.37	2.40
Answer the needs of the others	2.20	2.27

Table 7 shows that – in spite of other differences – both leftist and rightist voters are more concerned with solidarity and universalism than with other values. This confirms the observation of Loredana Sciolla that I discuss below, who underlines the point that, compared to some other European countries, Italians perform quite well in this regard.[15] Yet if the differences are not dramatic, nevertheless a clear difference emerges in Table 7 between Ulivo (the centre-left coalition) and Forza Italia (as Berlusconi's party was still called in 2006) voters. Ulivo voters seem more concerned with all the values around solidarity and equality, while Forza Italia addresses voters who believe, and are interested, in the values of consumption, wealth, success, and power. A large part of these values are strongly reflected in the most popular television programmes.

The values of individualised politics progressively replace the most traditional imagery of 'old' politics. *Who wants to be a Millionaire?* perfectly embodies the inner logic of individualisation. Yet the data in Table 7 show that a large part of Italian voters is still concerned with the values of solidarity and universalism.

Honesty is seen as a key value in most societies; indeed, much of the polemical argument around politics and politicians concerns issues of trust and truthfulness. Yet the data seem to show that the slighter interest in values of the common good and interest goes together with an equally slight attention to the honesty of the competing candidates.

---

[15] It has to consider also that answers to these and similar questions may be affected by different forms of wishful thinking: 'this is the answer that is expected'.

Table 8. % of respondents perceiving Prodi and Berlusconi as . . .

	Prodi	Berlusconi
Honest	58	24
Understanding people's problems	63	37
Trustworthy	50	37
Competent	61	54
Pleasant	44	42
Strong leader	44	89

As Table 8 shows, when asked about Berlusconi's honesty, only 24% believe that he is honest, against 58% who think that his opponent in the 2006 election, Prodi, is honest. Moreover, only 37% believe he is trustworthy against 50% who believe that Prodi is. What is defined as the 'dishonest vote' (the vote that is given to a candidate who is perceived as less honest that his opponent) is particularly strong among those who identify themselves as centre-right voters (Garcia, 2009).

Why was the one who is perceived as honest defeated at the polls by the one who is perceived as less honest? Is the 'honesty' category not sufficient to motivate voters? Are they motivated by other categories they consider of greater importance? Probably both factors are relevant: the 'honesty' category is not sufficient to win the election and there are other categories that motivate voters even more. There are also elements connected to the structure of the political system: electoral alliances, electoral system, local strategies that favour one candidate in the face of the other one, the weakness of the competing parties, and the absence of a strong leader of the centre-left coalition. But, at the end, there is no doubt that the 'honesty' category is not the determining one: a large part of Italian citizens are not that interested in honesty and, whatever their reasons, vote for the candidate who is perceived to be less honest.

In the last elections those who voted for PdL were 37.4% of Italian voters. The centre-right coalition (PdL, Lega Nord, and MPA) got 46.8% of all the votes. Does it mean that almost 50% of the Italian voters are not interested in honesty? Probably not: though here, too, there seems to emerge a general attitude more inclined towards individualism and particularism, an attitude that places less weight on the existing rules and on the idea of general interest. It is an attitude that confirms what Almond and Verba found in 1963:

the picture of Italian political culture that has emerged from our data is one of relatively unrelieved political alienation and of social isolation and distrust . . . Italians are particularly low in national pride, in moderate and open partisanship, in the acknowledgement of the obligation to take an active part in local community affairs, in their ability to join with the others in situations of political stress, in their choice of social forms of leisure-time activity, and in their confidence in the social environment. (Almond and Verba, 1963: 402)

Before Almond and Verba, Edward Banfield had reached very similar conclusions with his study in the south of Italy, and with his idea of 'amoral familism' (the extreme defence of family interests, with little care for moral values) opposed to the sense of belonging to a wider community (Banfield, 1958). Robert Putnam substantially confirmed this thesis thirty years after Almond and Verba, stressing the difficulty in acting together for the common interest that he observed in many Italian regions, especially in the south (Putnam, 1993). Many others would follow the same path: in 1998, discussing the characteristics of national identity, Ernesto Galli della Loggia writes: 'individualism, but also a very well rooted familialism: these are the two main characters of the Italian social being that are most often pointed out by foreign observers, but also by a long tradition of national self-consciousness' (1998: 87). For Galli della Loggia, the existence of different, and very often contrasting, familial sources of power is the reason for the more general distrust for rules of the entire community.

More recently, Loredana Sciolla, using data from the European Values Survey and World Values Survey, has found that, in the matter of 'civicness' (a positive attitude towards the rules of the community and the acceptance of social duties) in four countries (Italy, Spain, the United States, and France), today Italy comes third after the United States and Spain, with France in the last position. She notes also that in the last ten years there has been an important change and while 'civicness' has improved a lot in the United States and in Spain, so that Spain has overtaken Italy, it has instead declined in Italy (Sciolla, 2004). Is this a Berlusconi effect?

Conclusion: Is Television to be Blamed? Are the Italians Bad Guys?

I could end this discussion with the memory of the good old days: as always, it was much better then! It is fairly clear that no one likes the concept (the reality may be different) of the commodification of politics, and to see citizens reduced to passive spectators. It was *much better* when mass parties were playing a major function of organisers of consensus and representatives of interest. At the same time a critical image of Italian citizens emerges from what has been said in the last few pages. Do we have to blame television for the dismantling of the old values and imagery of traditional politics? And is this dismantling even more dramatic because of the low level of civicness of Italian citizens?

Berlusconi's style of politics highlights a process of change that is, in some measure, universal – even if it locates itself in the specificities of the Italian political culture. As Galli della Loggia has noted, the more general changes produced by television have to be inserted within a culture that, historically, appears more inclined to individualism than to shared values, to particularism than to universalism, to private solutions than to community decision-making.

Yet Berlusconi points us beyond Italy, and highlights a very general change in the structure of politics and its relationship to citizens. The old politics of the twentieth century is over; the 'great narratives', the broad and general ideological constructions that gave birth to the mass parties of the last century and that motivated the involvement of citizens with politics appear to have been overtaken by a continuous overlap between the political choices and imagery of everyday life. Citizens' exposure to the mass media generates a complex of symbols, values, dreams, aspirations within which politics is inserted: this complex and often contradictory framework refers essentially to individual life and its everyday problems.

This is a general tendency, not just an Italian one. The much-discussed issue of the progressive weakening of mass parties is relevant here: there seems to be a universal tendency that may take different forms in relationship to different social and political contexts. In Italy the progressive weakening of mass parties has left room for the identification of one single leader with a large proportion of Italian citizens – an identification based on shared values, far from traditional political values, in large part depending on habits of cultural consumption and on the particularistic attitudes within Italian civic life.

There is a large debate on populism and telepopulism: Berlusconi's populism is of course much discussed – but, mainly on the left, critics now discuss the concept of euro-populism (Biorcio, 2010) as it seems that all through Europe new cases of populism inhabit the political arena. The French sociologist Pierre Musso has talked about 'Sarkoberlusconisme', to stress the many similarities existing between the figure of the French President Nicolas Sarkozy and that of Berlusconi, between their political decisions, their policies but also between the ways in which they construct their relationship to citizens (Musso, 2008). 'Sarkoberlusconisme is a political phenomenon, even if it assembles, or distorts, methods drawn from marketing, business management and television . . . it mixes together the culture of business and the culture of the Church within a very strange combination of glorification of competitiveness and moralization of capitalism' (Musso, 2008: 30). Again, values that are not part of the traditional political environment now enter the political sphere. Musso too highlights that one needs to go beyond the specific cases of Berlusconi and Sarkozy and look for the more general lines of change that their specific cases reveal. The Sarkoberlusconisme, he writes, cannot be reduced to the populist, neo-populist, telepopulist interpretation, 'Sarkoberlusconisme is a renovated form of politics, it is a neo-politics' (Musso, 2008: 10).

The place that private life takes in the Sarkozy experience is very similar to the continuous references that Berlusconi makes to everyday language and experiences. Everyday life – and gossip column life – is to be found in Sarkozy's divorce of his previous wife, in the images of him hand in hand with Carla Bruni, his present wife, in front of the pyramids. And of course Sarkozy's marriage with the famous singer/model/beauty demonstrates how politics overlaps with spectacle and with stars. Both Berlusconi and Sarkozy can be defined as expressions of audience democracy: they put their bodies on the political stage through their private lives – lives that chime in with the widely popular imagery of the television and entertainment industry (Bobba, 2011).

'After the PM's photographer come the stylists?'[16] was a recent headline in the *Guardian*. It didn't apply to Berlusconi (nor to Sarkozy) but to the British Prime Minister David Cameron: both his personal photographer and 'brand stylist' have been hired as civil servants. When both Tony Blair and David Cameron entrusted past editors of tabloid papers with the responsibility of running their communication offices (though Andy Coulson, former editor of the *News of the World* and head of communications for Cameron, resigned early in 2011 as allegations increased that phone tapping of celebrities was widespread in the newspaper during his editorship) they clearly demonstrated the need to get closer to the everyday life of citizens, to their preferred readings and tastes. As Coleman suggests, they make an effort to bring the Big Brother house closer to the Houses of Parliament. They hire professionals who talk the language of the former while operating in the latter. They clearly understand that politics cannot be separated from the primary everyday cultural consumption of their fellow citizens.

So far, the idea of 'lifestyle politics' has been used to refer to consumption choices that carry a political meaning. Political consumerism has become the replacement for the diminishing role of political parties. What I am suggesting here goes further than that: lifestyle politics may also indicate the identification of citizens with the model of life proposed by *political* institutions and mainly by *political* actors. By voting for Berlusconi the citizen chooses what Berlsuconi is proposing as a model of everyday life. This citizen may pay only slight attention to the policy choices the Prime Minister offers: he looks essentially at the framework of values he himself embodies. Italian citizens pay more attention to the Berlusconi lifestyle than to his political programme that most will never read. His lifestyle fits perfectly with what Italian citizens see every day on the television screens. With his bandana, the present Italian Prime Minister is offering to those who walk along the streets of Porto Rotondo, and to the millions more who see his picture in newspapers and on the television screen, a style of life: as a political actor, he is asking his supporters and the public at large to vote for that particular lifestyle at least as much as for the political programme he proposes.

Is this populism? Defining Berlusconi (and then Sarkozy) as populist leaders would assume that there is a 'good' politics, the traditional politics

---

[16] *Guardian*, 6 Nov. 2010.

with its struggle over ideal visions of society, and on the other side there is its opposite, represented by those leaders and parties that put a representation of everyday life at the centre of their discourse. Defining Berlusconi as simply populist means not understanding that politics has changed, that in the face of the dramatic increase in the role of mass media, and television in particular, politics cannot remain the same. It has to adapt to the new tendencies of cultural consumption and therefore to the whole imagery of this now-dominant mode of life. As Musso puts it, we are facing a era of 'neo-politics' and any interpretation that revives the possible 'populist' interpretation risks being out of date.

Because of his experience as a television entrepreneur, Berlusconi has understood very well the changes now underway in cultural consumption, and how these changes could affect the relationship of citizens to politics.

Is commodification of politics another universal tendency? Commodification is undoubtedly the inner logic of most television programming everywhere in the world: most TV soap operas talk about success/defeat in business, most shows feature successful men/women, etc. This takes place everywhere in the world, not just in Italy: *Big Brother* is a Dutch invention, not an Italian one. Of course, more research is needed to check how many Berlusconis can appear in other parts of world, and under which circumstances. Other research is needed before we can definitively state without any doubt that commodification of politics and lifestyle politics are universal tendencies independent of contextual situations.

Commodification is the logic of British tabloids that narrate every day stories about the love affairs of attractive movie stars with successful football players, meeting in fancy hotels in beautiful sea resorts in the Caribbean or in Doha. Then on the third or fourth page there is an article on the struggle between Cameron and Clegg in forming a new government coalition. Are we sure it is possible to make a clear distinction between naked bodies on the beach at Santorini and MPs discussing policy in Westminster? From the tabloids, that every day mix together these two symbolic frameworks, came the communication heads of two recent British Prime Ministers, hired to bring into government their skills in addressing the everyday concerns of average citizens learned from addressing them for years though the tabloids. The reception of these messages, of this mixture between different social imageries, has much to do with national culture. In the Italian case, there is a national culture inclined towards individualism, particularism, and familism: thus, as our data show, the Prime Minister talks to a large percentage of Italians for whom personal benefit represents a very important value that comes before other, more traditional, political values, and before the more general interests of the entire community.

Berlusconi knew what he was talking about when he told his interviewer that most Italians want to be like him. Through his extensive use of research material, Berlusconi is able to know his citizens' attitudes and desires, and thus to offer a large part of these citizens what they want. He knows that, at root, people do not harbour traditional political values but more often values deriving from a cultural consumption much affected by television and other mass media discourses.

I do not know if, in writing about audience democracy, Manin had Berlusconi in mind: in any case, his thesis is very helpful in understanding better the latter's political offering. If we accept the idea of audience democracy, it seems necessary to include the world of politics, and the actions performed by its actors, within the more general symbolic framework of cultural consumption of the members of this audience. This framework is deeply shaped by the imagery that they see every day in the mass media: and politics has to be adapted to this prevailing framework. In Italy, even more than elsewhere, the prevailing medium is television. The experience of Berlusconi seems to suggest that the values of consumption may be strongly influenced by the way in which a large percentage of citizens perceive political and electoral involvement – a perception which has substantially, and quite rapidly, overcome what were the traditional political attitudes and loyalties. Italian individualism seems to foster a process of commodification of politics that Berlusconi and his television empire embody in an almost perfect way.

The progressive weakening of mass parties leaves room for a strong leader, in this case with enormous resources of money and media, who has been able to integrate his politics with the new framework of images and desires. These images are deeply rooted in the content of the mass media. At the same time this leader has met the expectations of a political culture increasingly strongly influenced by individualism and particularism. Seventeen years after Berlusconi publicly declared a union between politics and media, the feeling is still strong that commercial television has dramatically changed the idea and the structure of Italian politics.

Which lessons?

Italians went to the polls to vote for mayors and local government while I was finishing this essay: they also took part in a referendum which included questions on nuclear power and privatisation. In both cases the candidates and preferences of the centre-right were defeated. These were not national elections: the next general election need not take place until 2013. Yet many observers predicted, once the results were in, that the Berlusconi era is ending.

It may be: but the political adventure of 'Il Cavaliere' will leave an important mark. It shows that the traditional organisation of politics, both its public representation but also the way in which citizens play an active part in it, is over. Social change and new forms of cultural consumption, linked essentially to mass media in general and television in particular, are determining new forms of participation in the life of the community. Berlusconi has pushed this logic to an extreme and he has skilfully mixed the new media logic with rooted characteristics of Italian national identity. Other political options in other countries will find their own ways to adapt themselves to the new dominant patterns of cultural consumption and to the more general tendencies of social change: but Berlusconi will be a model, to emulate or avoid.

There are other lessons as well that we can learn from the Berlusconi case: first of all, as many observers have already pointed out, limits on the concentration of the mass media system are needed to allow a more equal and comprehensive pluralism. Because of a long history, and because of the well-rooted complexity of the Italian political system, these limits have always been lacking. Because of the well-established alliances between media corporations and political parties and groups that existed even before the beginning of the political adventure of Berlusconi, the Italian Parliament has not been able to reach an agreement on limiting the enormous concentration of media power in the hands of a single person.

The traditional overlap between mass media and politics, that has been for centuries a characteristic feature of the Italian public sphere, has prevented the adoption of any anti-concentration legislation in the field of mass media. Berlusconi has taken advantage of this absence, and he has been very happy to preserve it. Common wisdom about the political experience of 'Il Cavaliere' teaches this lesson.

The enormous power played by television (again, Berlusconi used this to his advantage) has been determined by the tradition of an elite print press that has driven many citizens, more than in other countries, towards the TV screen – because they didn't find their interests represented in Italian newspapers. For decades the reading of a newspaper was limited to an elite that, most of the time, was already socialised to politics: most were effectively excluded from this activity. As Enzo Forcella wrote in 1959 – metaphorically – the Italian newspapers readers were 'Millecinquecento' (one thousand five hundred) (Forcella, 1959): they are many more now: but the fact that the number is still limited goes a long way to explaining why, in Italy, television is the main 'agenda setter'.

The absence of a strong, independent journalism has had a double consequence. The development of the figure of a critical citizen has been prevented or delayed, because the idea of a common good beyond and above the competing interests of the country has not been fostered. Particularism, very diffused in society at large, has been increased by the absence of news media outlets which are not part of the ongoing political struggle and the specific (particularistic) interests that motivated most the investment in the media. If media partisanship can be an expression of external pluralism, it risks also fostering political polarisation within which the ideas of general interest and common good can get lost. Indeed, nobody, or very few organisations and citizens, was concerned to promote these ideas beyond stereotyped and banal declarations. The second consequence has been the progressive and continuous adaptation of citizens to a high level of mass media partisanship – such that it was not seen to be a scandal when Berlusconi decided to enter the political arena, and to use his own media outlets to support his candidacy.

New democracies, but well established ones too, may regard the Berlusconi case as a possible future development of their own traditions of democracy. This development carries all the risks linked to a cultural consumption depending on a market-driven system.

Berlusconi, his vision of politics quite distant from the traditional approach, is also the product of a political system which was substantially corrupt – and of a general public distrust towards all those who had some responsibility for government. When democracy and politics are not close to popular feelings and perceptions, the risk is that an 'outsider' can easily win the support of disappointed citizens with a vision constructed on commodification and lifestyle politics – as 'Il Cavaliere' has done. Many countries around the world show today a 'democratic deficit' (Norris, 2011) that may open the way to other Berlusconis.

Unfortunately, it seems that, more than fifteen years after Berlusconi first decided to enter the political arena, Italy has not learnt the lesson. Distrust (and corruption) still dominates the public sphere of the country.

References

Abruzzese, *Elogio del tempo nuovo: Perché Berlusconi ha vinto* (Genoa: Costa & Nolan, 1994).

G. Almond and S. Verba, *The Civic Culture: Political Attitudes and Democracy in Five Nations* (Princeton: Princeton University Press, 1963).

F. R. Ankersmit, *Aesthetic Politics* (Stanford, CA: Stanford University Press, 1996).

E. Banfield, *The Moral Basis of a Backward Society* (Chicago: Free Press, 1958).

D. Bell, The End of Ideology: On the Exhaustion of Political Ideas in the Fifties (Glencoe, IL: Free Press, 1960).

M. Belpoliti, *Il corpo del capo* (Parma: Guanda, 2009).

L. Bennet, 'The UnCivic Culture: Communication, Identity, and the Rise of Lifestyle Politics', *PS: Political Science and Politics*, 31/4 (1998), 740–61.

R. Biorcio, 'Europa, vento populista', *Reset* (Nov.–Dec. 2010).

G. Bobba, *Media e politica in Italia e in Francia: Due democrazie del pubblico a confronto* (Milan: Angeli, 2011).

N. Bobbio, *La sinistra nell'epoca del Karaoke* (Rome: I libri di Reset, 1994).

G. Bocca, Piccolo Cesare (Milan: Feltrinelli, 2002).

M. Calise, Il partito personale (Bari: Laterza, 2000).

D. Campus, L'antipolitica al governo (Bologna: Il Mulino, 2006).

–– 'Mediatization and Personalization of Politics in Italy and in France: The Cases of Berlusconi and Sarkozy', International Journal of Press/Politics 15/2 (2010), 219–35.

E. Caniglia, Berlusconi, Perot e Collor come political outside (Soveria Mannelli: Rubbettino, 2000).

P. Catellani and P. Milesi, 'Successo o benevolenza? I valori degli elettori', in Itanes (ed.), Dov'è la vittoria (Bologna: Il Mulino, 2006).

Censis and Ucsi (eds), Le diete mediatiche degli italiani nello scenario europeo (Milan: Angeli, 2006).

S. Coleman, 'A Tale of Two Houses: The House of Commons, the Big Brother House and the People at Home', *Parliamentary Affairs*, 56 (2003), 733–58.

−− and J. Blumler (2009) *The Internet and Democratic Citizenship* (Cambridge: Cambridge University Press).

J. Corner, 'Mediated Persona and Political Culture', in J. Corner and D. Pels (eds), *Media and the Restyling of Politics* (London: Sage, 2003).

P. Dahlgren, 'Media, Citizenship and Civic Culture', in J. Curran and M. Gurevitch (eds), *Mass Media and Society* (London: Arnold, 2000).

A. Dal Lago, 'Il voto e il circo', *Micromega*, 1 (1994).

J. de Beus, 'Audience Democracy: An Emerging Pattern in Post Modern Political Communication', in K. Brants and K. Voltmer (eds), *Political Communication in Postmodern Democracy: Challenging the Primacy of Politics* (New York: Palgrave Macmillan, 2011).

G. Debord, *La Societé du spectacle* (Paris: Editions Gerard Lebovici, 1967).

M. Delli Carpini and B. Williams, 'Let us Infotain you: Politics in the New Media Environment', in L. Bennet and R. Entmann (eds), *Mediated Politics* (Cambridge: Cambridge University Press, 2001).

I. Diamanti, 'La politica come marketing', *Micromega*, 2 (1994).

−− 'Prefazione', in B. Manin, *Principi del governo rappresentativo* (Bologna: Il Mulino, 2010).

J. Dunn, *Interpreting Political Responsibility* (Cambridge: Polity, 1990).

M. Edelman, *Politics as Symbolic Action* (Chicago: Markham Publishing Co., 1971).

−− *The Symbolic Uses of Politics* (Chicago: University of Illinois Press, 1976).

−− *Political Language: Words that Succeed and Policies that Fail* (New York: Academic Press, 1977).

−− *Constructing the Political Spectacle* (Chicago and London: University of Chicago Press, 1988).

S. Fabbrini, *Il Principe democratico* (Bari: Laterza, 1999).

A. Ferrara, 'Questo malanno non vi riguarda più di tutti?', *Reset*, 123 (Jan.–Feb. 2011), 31–6.

E. Forcella, 'Millecinquecento lettori', *Tempo presente*, 6 (1959).

F. Fukuyama, *The End of History and the Last Man* (London: Hamish Hamilton, 1992).

E. Galli della Loggia, *L'identità nazionale* (Bologna: Il Mulino, 1998).

D. Garcia, 'The Dishonest Vote in the Italian Election of 2006', paper presented to the XXIII Conference of Società Italiana di Scienza Politica, Rome, 17–19 Sept. 2009.

A. Gibelli, *Berlusconi passato alla storia* (Rome: Donzelli, 2010).

P. Ginsborg, *Silvio Berlusconi: Television, Power and Patrimony* (London and New York: Verso, 2004).

E. Green, *The Eyes of the People* (Oxford: Oxford University Press, 2010).

D. Hallin and P. Mancini, *Comparing Media Systems: Three Models of Media and Politics* (Cambridge: Cambridge University Press, 2004).

R. Inglehart, *Modernization and Postmodernization: Cultural, Economic and Political Change in Forty-Three Societies* (Princeton: Princeton University Press, 1997).

Itanes (ed.), *Perché ha vinto il centro-destra* (Bologna: Il Mulino, 2001).

Itanes (ed.), *Dov'è la vittoria* (Bologna: Il Mulino, 2006).

J. Jones, *Entertaining Politics* (Lanham, MD: Rowman & Littlefield, 2005).

R. Katz and P. Mair (eds), *How Parties Organize* (London: Sage, 1994).

O. Kirkheimer, 'The Transformation of West European Party Systems', in J. LaPalombara and M. Weiner (eds), *Political Parties and Political Development* (Princeton: Princeton University Press, 1964).

K. Land and G. Lang, 'The Television Personality in Politics: Some Considerations', *Public Opinion Quarterly*, 20/1 (1956), 103–12.

A. Langer, 'A Historical Exploration of the Personalization of Politics in the Print Media: The British Prime Minister 1945–1999', *Parliamentary Affairs*, 60/3 (2007), 371–87.

G. Legnante and G. Sani, 'Una breve campagna elettorale', in Itanes (ed.), *Il ritorno di Berlusconi* (Bologna: Il Mulino, 2008).

J. F. Lyotard, *La Condition postmoderne: Rapport sur le savoir* (Paris: Editions de Minuit, 1979).

P. Mair, *The West European Party System* (Oxford: Oxford University Press, 1990).

P. Mancini, *La maratona di Prodi e lo sprint di Berlusconi* (Rome: Carocci, 2007).

B. Manin, *The Principles of Representative Government* (Cambridge: Cambridge University Press, 1997).

M. Maraffi, 'Chi ha votato chi?', in Itanes (ed.), *Il ritorno di Berlusconi* (Bologna: Il Mulino, 2008).

D. Marshall, *Celebrity and Power* (Minneapolis: University of Minnesota Press, 1997).

G. Mazzoleni and W. Schulz, 'Mediatization of Politics: A Challenge for Democracy?', *Political Communication*, 16/3 (1999), 247–63.

— and A. Sfardini, *Politica Pop: Da 'Porta a Porta' a 'L'Isola dei famosi'* (Bologna: Il Mulino, 2009).

— J. Stewart, and B. Horsfield, *The Media and Neo-Populism* (Westport, CT: Praeger, 2003).

Y. Meny and Y. Surel (eds), *Democracies and the Populist Challenge* (New York: Palgrave, 2002).

T. Meyer with L. Hinchman, *Media Democracy: How the Media Colonize Politics* (Cambridge: Polity, 2002).

M. Micheletti, *Political Virtues and Shopping: Individuals, Consumerism and Collective Action* (New York: Palgrave, 2003).

E. Miller-Jones, *Silvio Berlusconi: Flamboyant Politics and Massive Wealth* (Beau Bassin: VDM Publishing House, 2011).

A. Mughan, *Media and the Presidentialization of Parliamentary Elections* (New York: Palgrave, 2000).

P. Musso, *Le Sarkoberlusconisme* (Paris: Editions de l'Aube, 2008).

P. Norris, *Democratic Deficit: Critical Citizens Revisited* (Cambridge: Cambridge University Press, 2011).

A. Panebianco, *Political Parties: Organization and Party* (Cambridge: Cambridge University Press, 1988).

A. Parisi and G. Pasquino, 'Relazioni partiti elettori et tipi di voto', in A. Parisi and G. Pasquino (eds), *Continuità e mutamento elettorale in Italia* (Bologna: Il Mulino, 1977).

P. P. Pasolini, *Scritti corsari* (Milan: Garzanti, 1975).

D. Pels, 'Aesthetic Representation and Political Style: Re-balancing Identity and Difference in Media Democracy', in J. Corner and D. Pels (eds), *Media and the Restyling of Politics* (London: Sage, 2003).

Y. Peri, *Telepopulism* (Stanford, CA: Stanford University Press, 2004).

G. Pilo, *Perchè il Polo ha perso le elezioni* (Rome: Newton Compton, 1996).

A. Pizzorno, *Il potere dei giudici : Stato democratico e controllo della virtù* (Bari: Laterza, 1998).

T. Poguntke and P. Webb (eds), *The Presidentialization of Politics* (New York: Oxford University Press, 2005).

E. Poli, *Forza Italia: Strutture, leadership e radicamento territorial* (Bologna: Il Mulino, 2001).

N. Postman, *Amusing Ourselves to Death* (New York: Penguin, 1985).

R. Putnam, *Making Democracy Work* (Princeton: Princeton University Press, 1993).

L. Ricolfi, 'Elezioni e mass media: Quanti voti ha spostato la TV', *Il Mulino*, 43 (1994), 775–800.

K. Riegert (ed.), *Politicotainment: Television's Take on the Real* (New York: Lang, 2007).

G. Russo, *Perchè la sinistra ha eletto Berlusconi* (Milan: Sperling & Kupfer, 1994).

G. Sartori, *Homo videns* (Bari: Laterza, 2000).

R. G. Schwartzenberg, *L'Etat Spectacle* (Paris: Flammarion, 1977).

L. Sciolla, *La sfida dei valori* (Bologna: Il Mulino, 2004).

B. Severgnini, *La pancia degli italiani* (Milan: Rizzoli, 2010).

D. Shah *et al.* (2007) Political Consumerism: How Communication and Consumption Orientations Drive 'Life Style Politics', in *The Annals of the American Academy of Political and Social Science* (611), p. 217–35

A. Shehata and J. Strömbäck, 'A Matter of Context: A Comparative Study of Media Environment and News Consumption Gaps in Europe', *Political Communication*, 28/1 (2011), 110–34.

A. Stille, *Citizen Berlusconi* (Milan: Garzanti, 2006).

D. Swanson and P. Mancini (eds), *Politics, Media and Modern Democracy* (Westport, CT: Praeger, 1996).

P. Sylos Labini, *Berlusconi e gli anticorpi: Diario di un cittadino indignato* (Bari: Laterza, 2003).

C. Trigilia, *Le subculture politiche territoriali* (Milan: Feltrinelli, 1981).

L. van Zoonen, *Entertaining the Citizen* (Lanham, MD: Rowman & Littlefield, 2005).

E. Veltri and M. Travaglio, *L'odore dei soldi* (Rome: Editori Riuniti, 2001).

WAN (ed.), *World Press Trends* (Paris: WAN, 2009).

Acknowledgments

I would like to thank David Levy and John Lloyd for their patience and help. I am also indebted to Jan Zielonka for giving me the opportunity to get in touch with the stimulating environment of the University of Oxford and for his continuous support and advice. A special thanks also to the Reuters Institute and the Department of Politics and International Relations at the University of Oxford for making possible much of the research included in this book.

Paolo Mancini

Paolo Mancini is Professor in the Department of Institutions and Society at the University of Perugia. He has served as a visiting professor at the University of California, San Diego, and in 1995 he was a Fellow at the Shorenstein Center at Harvard University. In 2001 Mancini was a Fellow at the Erik Brost Institute, University of Dortmund, and in 2009 was at St. Antony's College, University of Oxford. His major publications include *Politics, Media and Modern Democracy* with David Swanson, *Il sistema fragile; Sociologie della comunicazione* with Alberto Abruzzese and *Elogio della lottizzazione*. In 2004, with Daniel C. Hallin, he co-authored *Comparing Media Systems: Three Models of Media and Politics*, which won the Goldsmith Book Award (2005) from Harvard University, the Diamond Anniversary Book Award of the National Communication Association (2005) and the Outstanding Book Award of the International Communication Association (2006).